BRANCH LINES TO HENLEY WINDSOR AND MARLOW

Vic Mitchell and Keith Smith

Middleton Press

Cover picture: 0-6-0PT no. 9403 is about to leave Henley-on-Thames for Twyford at 4.4pm on 21st April 1957. This was almost the ultimate development of the Pannier Tank design. (B.W.Leslie/GWS)

Published February 2002

ISBN 1 901706 77 X

© Middleton Press, 2002

Design   Deborah Esher
Typesetting Barbara Mitchell

Published by
       Middleton Press
       Easebourne Lane
       Midhurst, West Sussex
       GU29 9AZ
Tel: 01730 813169
Fax: 01730 812601

Printed & bound by Biddles Ltd,
       Guildford and Kings Lynn

CONTENTS

Henley-on-Thames branch	1-37
Windsor branch	38-76
Maidenhead to High Wycombe	77-109
Marlow branch	110-120

INDEX

92	Bourne End		112	Marlow
88	Cookham		17	Shiplake
85	Furze Platt		38	Slough
24	Henley-on-Thames		1	Twyford
107	High Wycombe		12	Wargrave
104	Loudwater		57	Windsor & Eton Central
77	Maidenhead		102	Wooburn Green

ACKNOWLEDGEMENTS

Our sincere gratitude goes to so many of the photographers who have helped us and also to P.G.Barnes, A.E.Bennett, W.R.Burton, R.M.Casserley, G.Croughton, D.Edge, M.J.Furnell, B.Gilbert, J.C.Gillham, G.Heathcliffe, J.B.Horne, N.Langridge, D.Mitchell, R.C.Riley, Mr D. and Dr. S.Salter, E.Youldon and especially our wives.

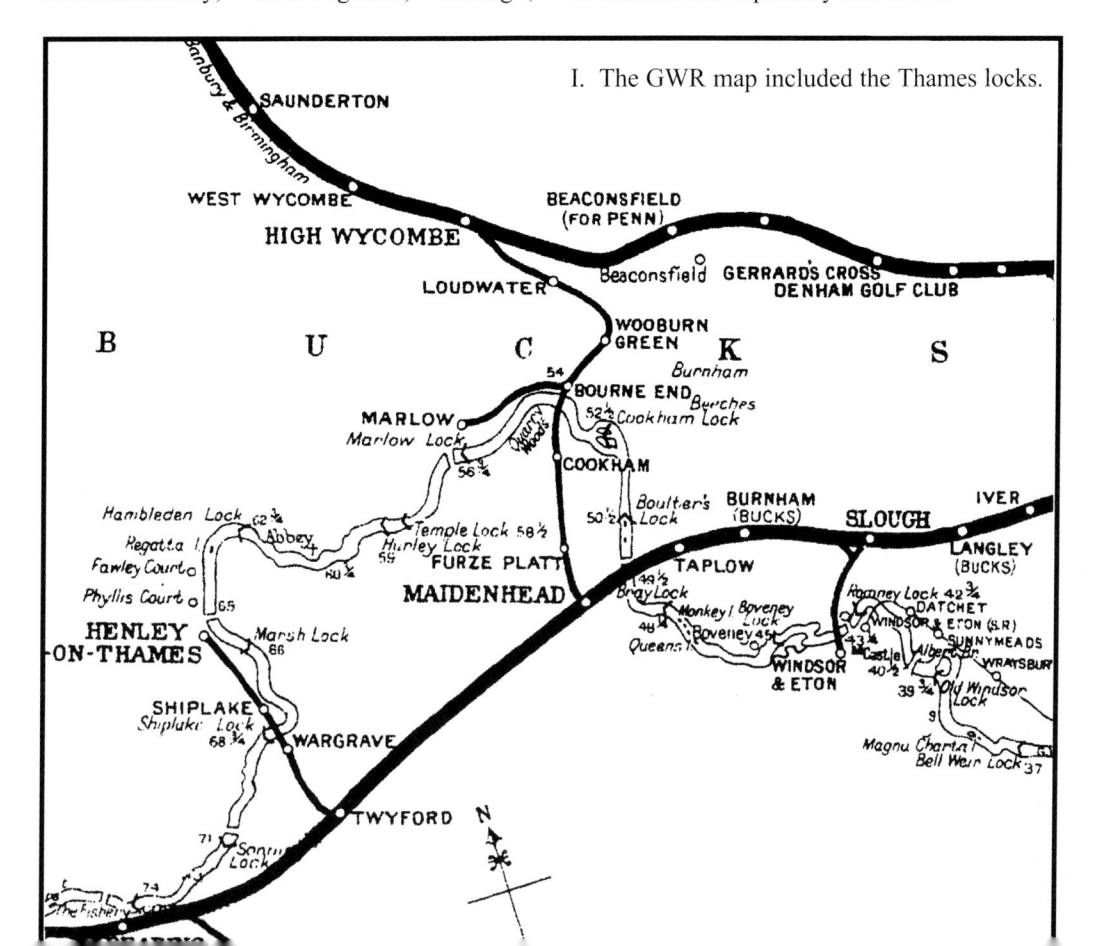

I. The GWR map included the Thames locks.

GEOGRAPHICAL SETTING

All the lines are closely related to the River Thames, except the Bourne End to High Wycombe section which was close to one of its tributaries, the River Wye.

The Windsor branch crosses the Thames Valley and is thus mainly on Alluvium. The other routes are mostly on the Chalk of the dip slope of the Chilterns, although this is extensively overlaid by superficial deposits of Gravel and Alluvium.

High Wycombe has a long association with the paper and furniture industries, resulting from its location in the well-wooded Chilterns. Slough is noted for its light industries, which have proliferated in the railway era. The other towns have strong associations with leisure activities, notably those involving the river, and tourism particularly at Windsor on account of its historic castle. This was built on an isolated outcrop of Chalk.

All the maps are at 25ins to 1 mile, unless otherwise described. North is at the top except where there is an arrow.

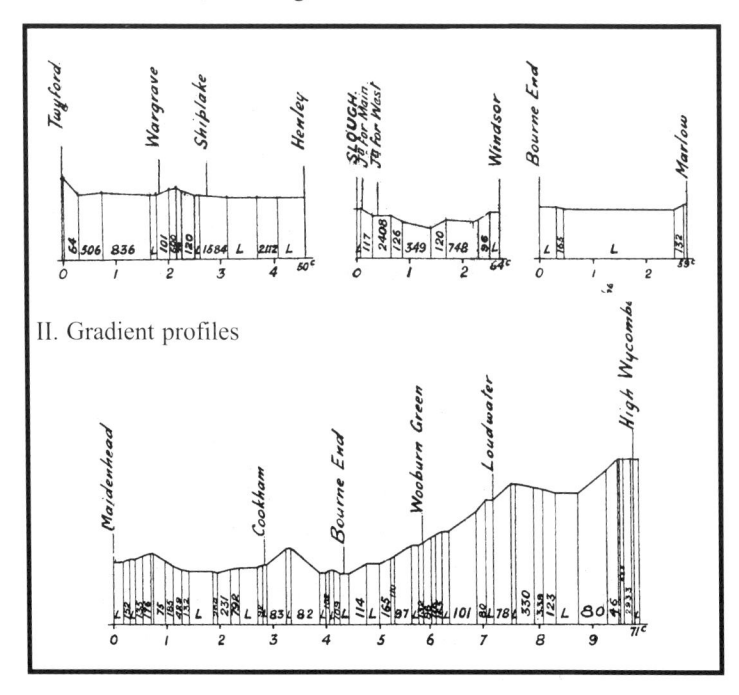

II. Gradient profiles

HISTORICAL BACKGROUND

The Great Western Railway's main line was opened between Paddington and Maidenhead on 4th June 1838, although neither station was on its present site. The line was extended to Twyford on 1st July 1839 and to Reading on 3rd March 1840.

The GWR branch to Windsor was opened on 10th October 1849, its Act having been secured in 1848.

The Wycombe Railway obtained an Act in 1846 to build a line from Maidenhead to High Wycombe. This single line was opened on 1st August 1854 and was operated by the GWR, which absorbed it in 1867. The route had been extended to Thame in 1862.

The Act for the Henley branch was passed on 27th July 1847 and traffic commenced on 1st June 1857.

The Great Marlow Railway was authorised on 13th July 1868 and the branch from the Wycombe Railway opened on 28th June 1873. It was worked by the GWR, but the company remained independent until 1897.

All the branches (except the latter) were

built to the main line gauge of 7ft 0¼ins. Standard gauge trains began thus: to Henley on 25th March 1876 and to High Wycombe on 2nd September 1870. The Windsor branch received a third rail on 1st March 1862 and was mixed gauge until 30th June 1883.

The Henley branch was doubled on 11th July 1898 as part of an unsuccessful plan to link it to the Marlow line and double track was provided to Windsor from the outset. Singling of the former took place on 20th June 1961 and the latter on 9th September 1963.

A more direct route between London and High Wycombe via Greenford was brought into traffic on 2nd April 1906 and the line from Maidenhead then became the equivalent of a backwater.

With the advent of nationalisation in 1948, the area became part of the Western Region of British Railways. The main economy measure later implemented was the closure of the line between Bourne End and High Wycombe on 4th May 1970.

Privatisation resulted in a 7½ year franchise being let on 13th October 1996, rolling stock and the branches being branded Thames Trains.

III. The Wycombe Railway is featured, together with the later surrounding developments.

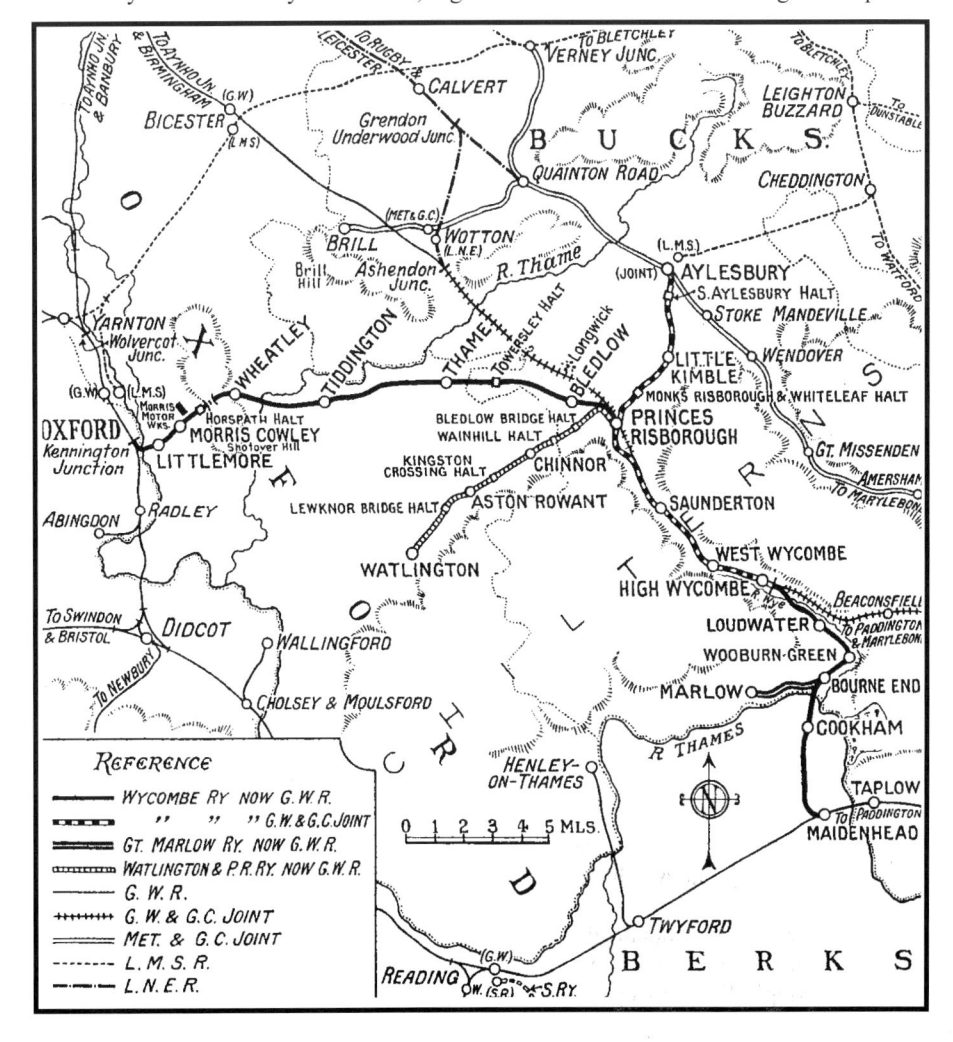

PASSENGER SERVICES

Only the weekday services are discussed, the Sunday timetable generally showing fewer trains on most of the branches. However, as leisure time increased the trains on such holidays in the Summer were often greatly increased in number.

Henley-on-Thames Branch

The initial timetable offered five return trips on the branch, this increasing to eight by 1868. The year 1900 brought the introduction of the first non-stop train to Paddington. Two years later, there were five through trains from London, one being a portion of a down express slipped at speed before reaching Twyford.

A service of about 20 trains per day was provided for most of the 20th century. Many ran to and from Reading but this convenience was curtailed in September 1974. However, an hourly off-peak service was restored on 14th June 1993. Direct trains to Paddington were also provided again from that date.

Windsor Branch

The first timetable listed eleven departures for Paddington. Some trains terminated at Victoria from 1863 and others continued from Paddington (Bishop's Road) to Farringdon Street on the Metropolitan Railway. Some up trains dropped slip coaches into Paddington before going underground. (A quick acting signalman was needed!)

By 1865 there were 29 arrivals at Windsor, 19 of which had started at one of the London stations mentioned. Branch trains carried slip coaches originating at London (two daily), Reading and also Plymouth.

In 1884-85, there were some through trains to and from the City via the District Railway, but the overall number of branch trains changed little for most of the remainder of that century.

By 1909, there were 39 down arrivals, including one from Basingstoke. Down trains had increased to 43 by 1928, but this was cut to 32 during much of World War II and some years subsequently.

By the mid-1950s, the figure had returned to around 40, which included 5 or 6 through London trains. A slow decline started in 1963 and by the end of that decade there was only one Paddington train. However, a regular 30-minute off-peak shuttle was introduced in 1960.

The last normal link with London ran on 30th April 1976, but a single down train was reintroduced in June 1993, for the benefit of tourists.

Maidenhead to High Wycombe

From the outset several trains ran to and from Paddington, a feature of timetables until 1970. A few used Victoria in the last quarter of the 19th century. There were eleven London trains in such widely separated dates as 1872 and 1938.

At the northern end of the route, a few trains continued to Oxford or Aylesbury. There was still a Maidenhead - Aylesbury service as late as May 1969.

For the last 30 years or so there has been a basic hourly service, most trains continuing to Marlow, but infrequently to London. The latter had one down and three up in 2001 for example.

Marlow Branch

Below are sample train frequencies.

1873	10
1902	12
1910	16
1938	23
1947	21
1972	20
2001	21

Until 1970, most trains simply shuttled to and from Bourne End, and London services were rare. In part of the 1890s, a coach was slipped from the 5.15pm from Paddington at Taplow and worked forward to Marlow.

Since 1970, the majority of trains have originated at Maidenhead. In recent years, the peak hour services have involved one train working four return trips on the branch, passengers having to change at Bourne End into another shuttling to Maidenhead.

1. Henley Branch

IV. The 1945 edition at 1ins to 1 mile reveals the relationship of the intermediate stations to the communities they serve. The River Thames forms the Oxon/Berks county boundary, which is represented by dots and dashes.

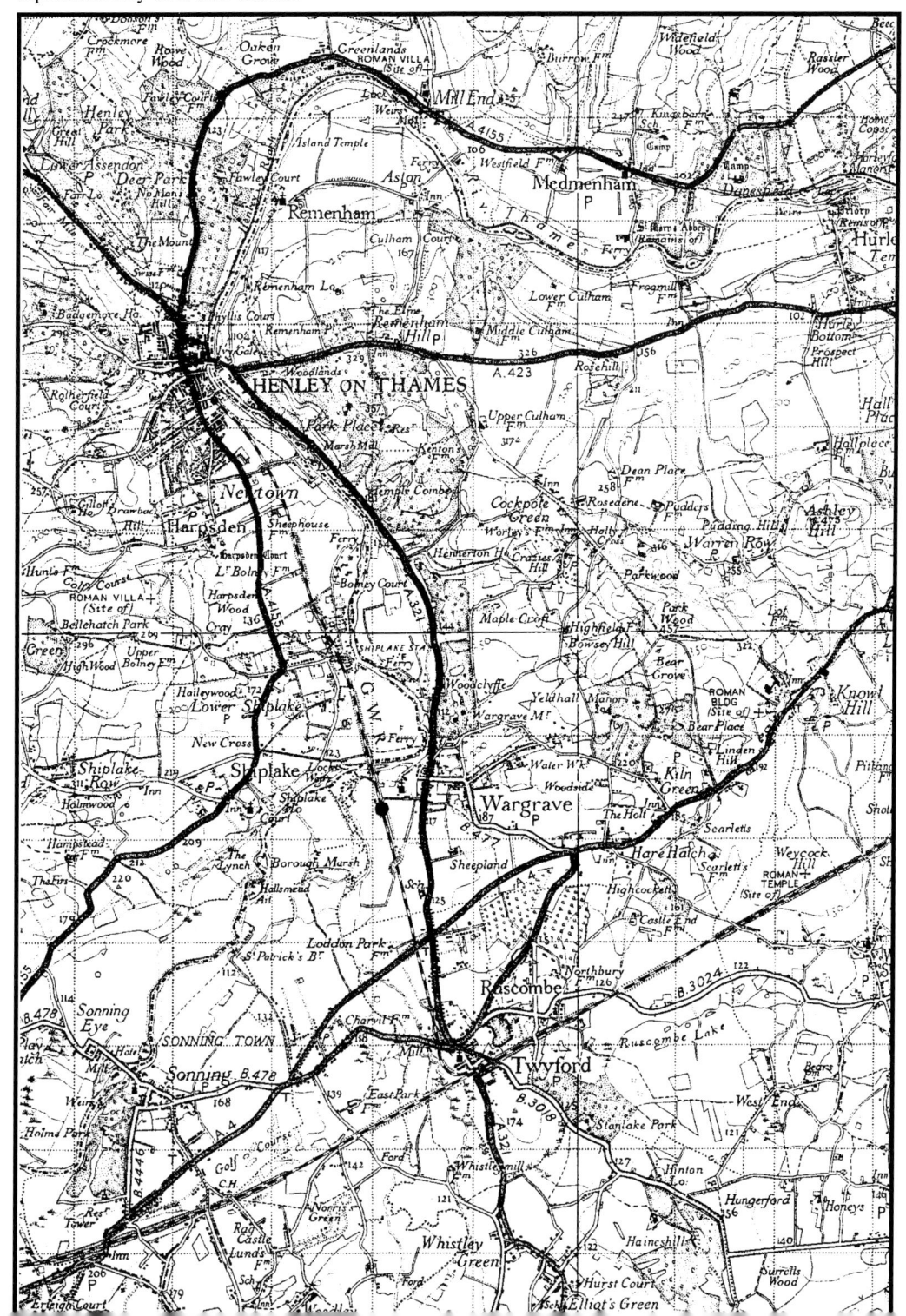

TWYFORD

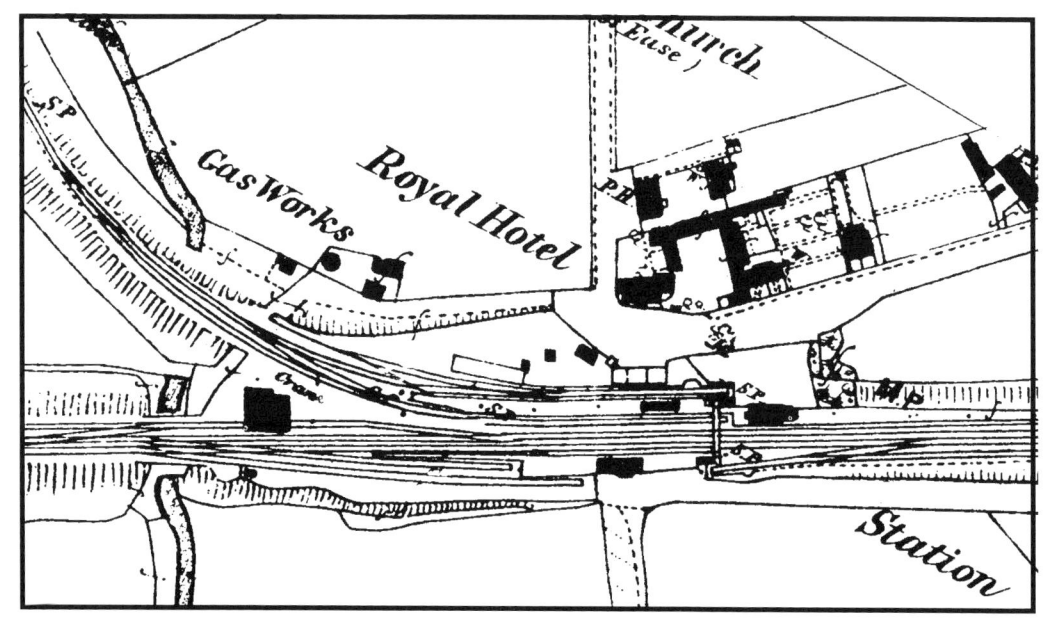

V.   The 1st edition of 1872 has the double track main line across the page, with a parallel siding each side of the station. The cartographer has failed to mark the connection to the branch. The small gasworks was in use between about 1858 and 1923; it was recorded as having consumed 686 tons of coal in 1912. Its site was used as a government fuel store in WWII.

1.   The quadrupling of 1893 was achieved here by the provision of the extra tracks on the south side (right). The connection from them to the branch (left) was by means of crossovers beyond the brick arch, near East Box. (Lens of Sutton)

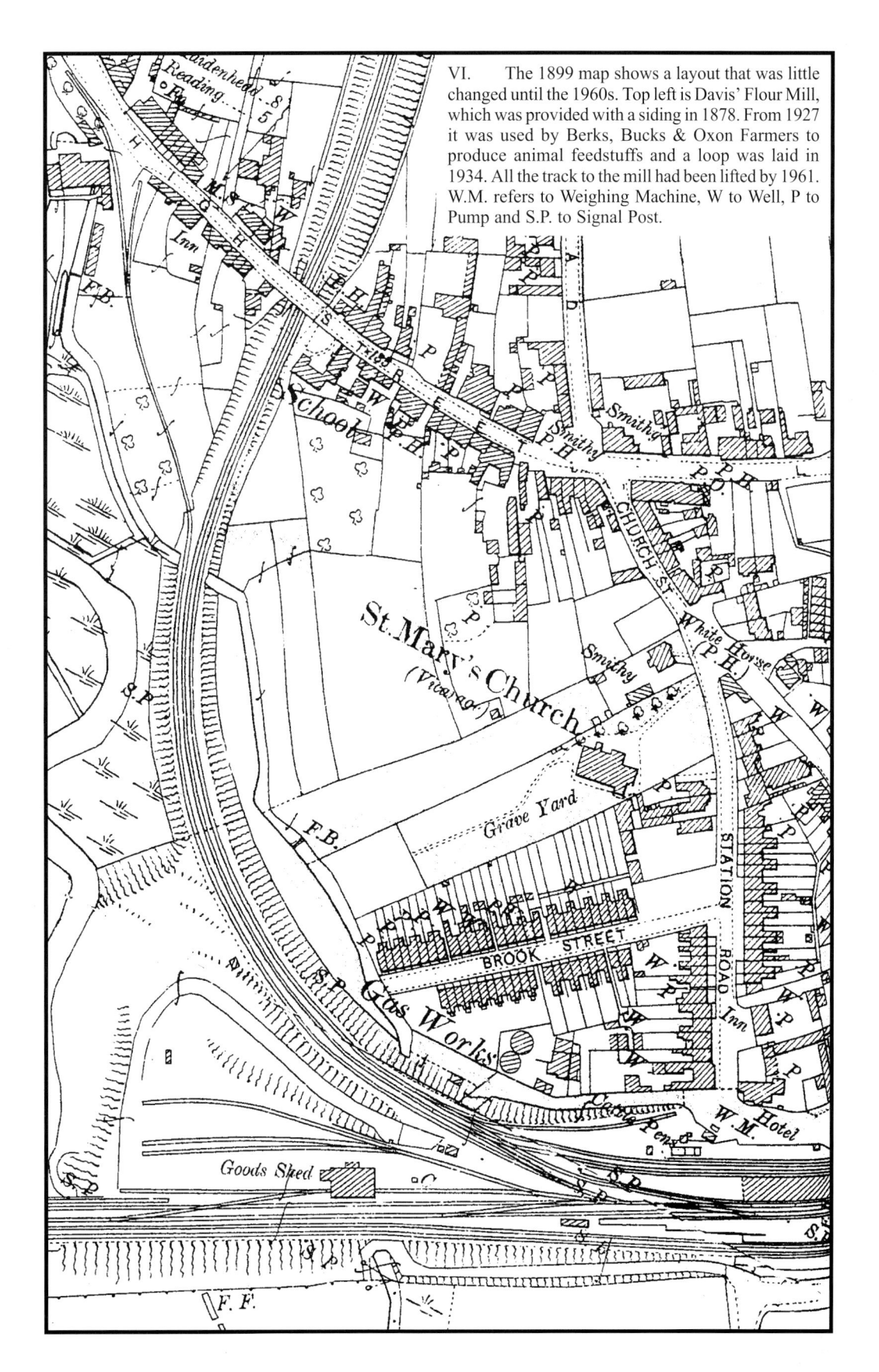

VI. The 1899 map shows a layout that was little changed until the 1960s. Top left is Davis' Flour Mill, which was provided with a siding in 1878. From 1927 it was used by Berks, Bucks & Oxon Farmers to produce animal feedstuffs and a loop was laid in 1934. All the track to the mill had been lifted by 1961. W.M. refers to Weighing Machine, W to Well, P to Pump and S.P. to Signal Post.

2.   The position of the points indicates that this 1076 "Buffalo" class 0-6-0ST and its train has come round the curve from the branch. In the background is West Box and the goods shed. The down connection to the branch was removed in 1972 in favour of a crossover behind the camera. (Lens of Sutton)

3.   A westward panorama in 1919 features the facilities provided in 1893. The previous station was also brick-built, but the original one was of timber construction. There was a staff of 28 recorded in 1923. (LCGB/NRM)

4. The GWR pioneered the diesel railcar in the UK and this was one of the first batch of 16 which began service in 1934. It was photographed in the bay in 1954. The second group had full size buffers; all had AEC engines. (I.D.Beale)

> **Other views of this station can be seen in pictures 40 to 48 in our *Slough to Newbury* album.**

5. Passengers alight from a Paddington to Reading train on 14th December 1985 and some will cross the left part of the bridge to join the train seen in the next picture. Few trains stopped at the two platforms on the right. (C.L.Caddy)

6. The branch train that day was formed of a railcar painted the GWR colours of chocolate and cream. Only one was so treated and this was done as part of the celebrations for the 150th anniversary of the formation of that company. (C.L.Caddy)

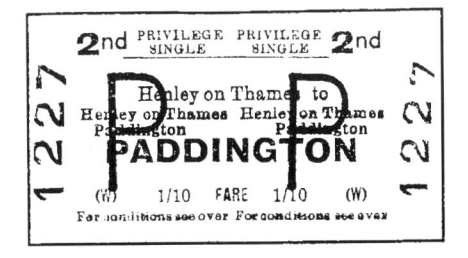

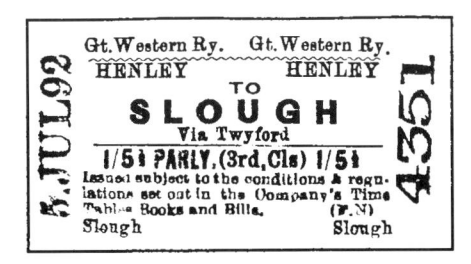

7. The car park was created on the site of the goods yard, which closed on 7th September 1964. Motorists reach the platform by using a foot crossing over the branch; the gate is open. No. 165127 is running from Henley to Reading on 10th November 1994 and will use the up relief line for over half a mile before crossing to the down one. (F.Hornby)

8. The main entrance and ticket office is on the north side of the station. The L-shaped canopy makes a distinctive feature; it carried an obsolete sign when photographed in 2000. (V.Mitchell)

9. Bicycles crowd the unusually curved up local platform as no. 59004 *Paul A.Hammond* approaches with a stone train from Somerset on 27th July 2000. The station was smart with well-kept gardens. (V.Mitchell)

10. The ambience was spoilt by signs of neglect by Railtrack. There was an engine release crossover here until 1961 and the dock siding was still in place in 1966. Both signal boxes were closed on 23rd October 1961 and were superseded by one on the car park site. This box had 56 levers and was in use until 20th March 1972. (V.Mitchell)

NORTH OF TWYFORD

11. No. 5763 approaches Twyford on 28th October 1951 and is about to pass the fogmans hut. In front of it is a telephone box and a lever to place three detonators on the rail. (J.H.Meredith)

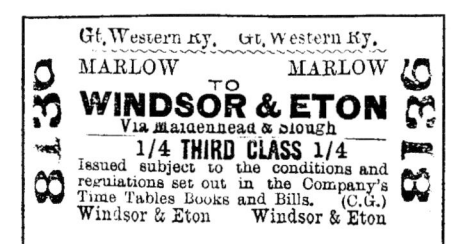

WARGRAVE

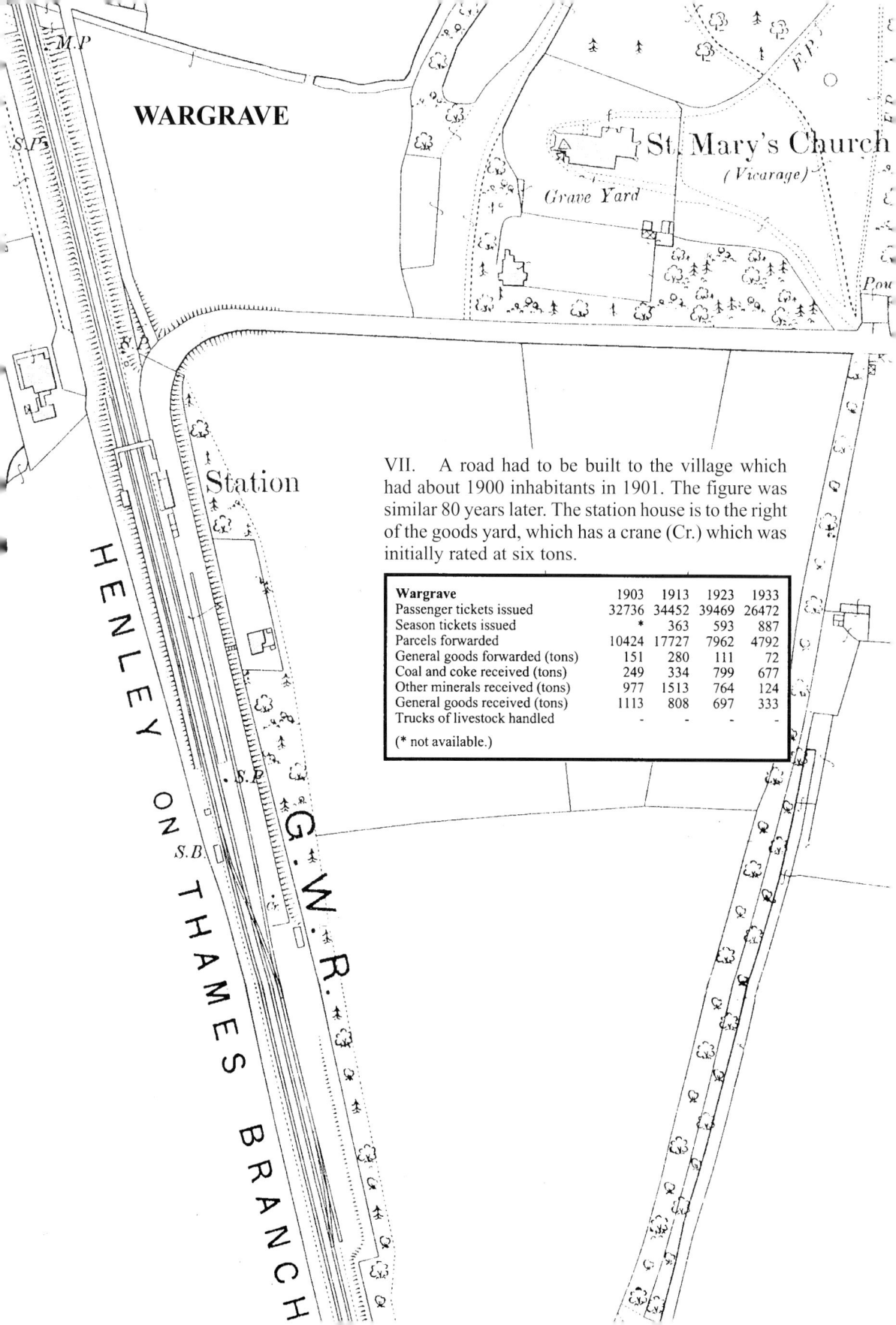

St. Mary's Church
(Vicarage)
Grave Yard

Station

HENLEY ON THAMES BRANCH G.W.R.

VII. A road had to be built to the village which had about 1900 inhabitants in 1901. The figure was similar 80 years later. The station house is to the right of the goods yard, which has a crane (Cr.) which was initially rated at six tons.

Wargrave	1903	1913	1923	1933
Passenger tickets issued	32736	34452	39469	26472
Season tickets issued	*	363	593	887
Parcels forwarded	10424	17727	7962	4792
General goods forwarded (tons)	151	280	111	72
Coal and coke received (tons)	249	334	799	677
Other minerals received (tons)	977	1513	764	124
General goods received (tons)	1113	808	697	333
Trucks of livestock handled	-	-	-	-

(* not available.)

12. The station opened on 1st October 1900 and was provided with a cantilevered canopy which avoided the need for platform stanchions. Four or five men were employed here for the station's first 40 years. (Lens of Sutton)

13. A 1921 southward panorama includes the down waiting room which has its seats temporarily on the platform. The small goods yard (centre) had a 3-ton crane latterly and was in use until 7th September 1964. Mail bags were brought from the village and milk churns from the surrounding farms. The shed near the 19-lever signal box was for lamps and oil. (LGRP/NRM)

14. This stylish ex-GWR railcar was photographed in the early fifties. A camping coach (or two) was positioned by the loading dock in the summers of 1936-39 and 1953-64. The signal box probably opened on 2nd January 1901, but closed certainly on 3rd October 1954. Apart from the early years, it was only manned during the busy Henley Regatta week. (Lens of Sutton)

15. The bicycle shed (left) arrived in 1946, as the original one was too small. This second generation railcar is bound for Twyford on 15th May 1966. The buildings were demolished in December 1985, having been staffed only part-time for almost 20 years. (C.L.Caddy)

16. There were no entrance doors from the approach road, passengers having to use the gateway onto the platform to gain access. The nearest shed was provided in 1901 for cycles, its neighbour being older and used for parcels. The footbridge was lost during the 1961 singling and only a small shelter is now provided. (C.L.Caddy)

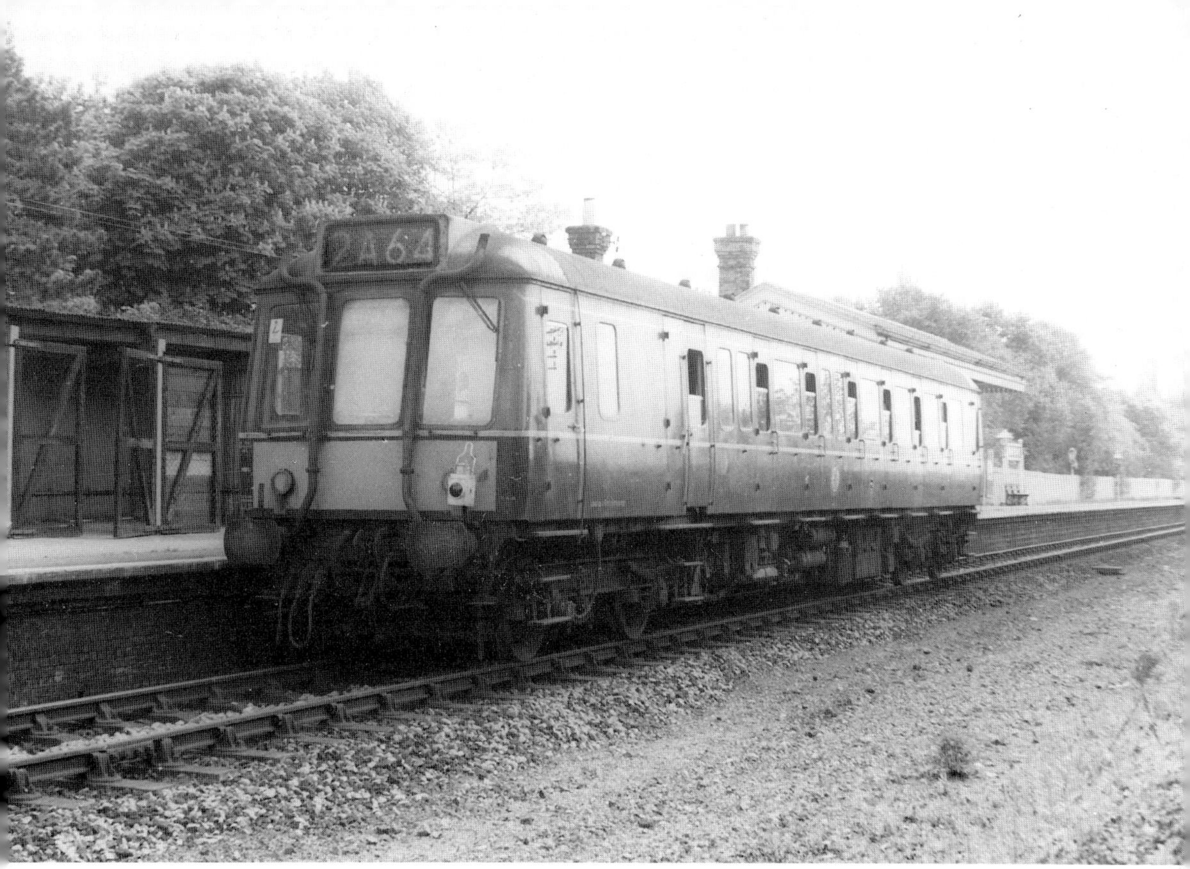
2A64

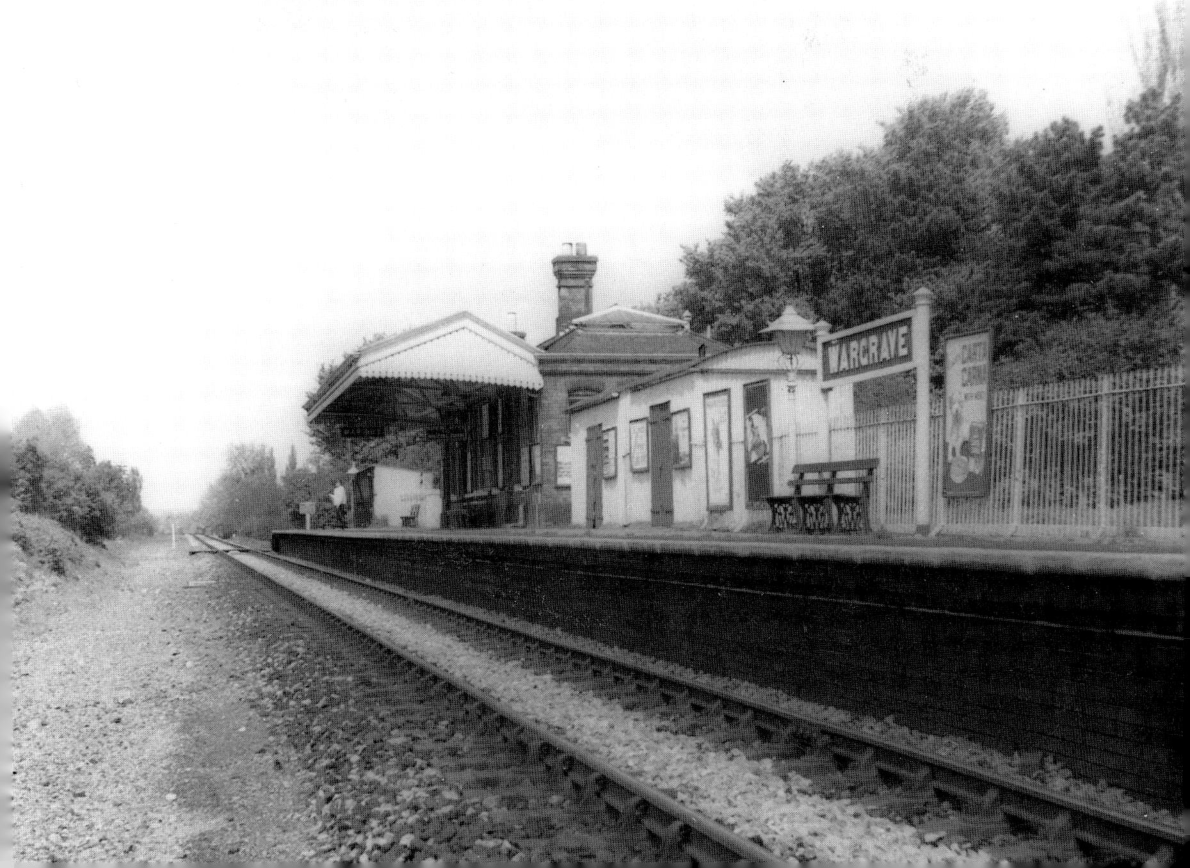
WARGRAVE

SHIPLAKE

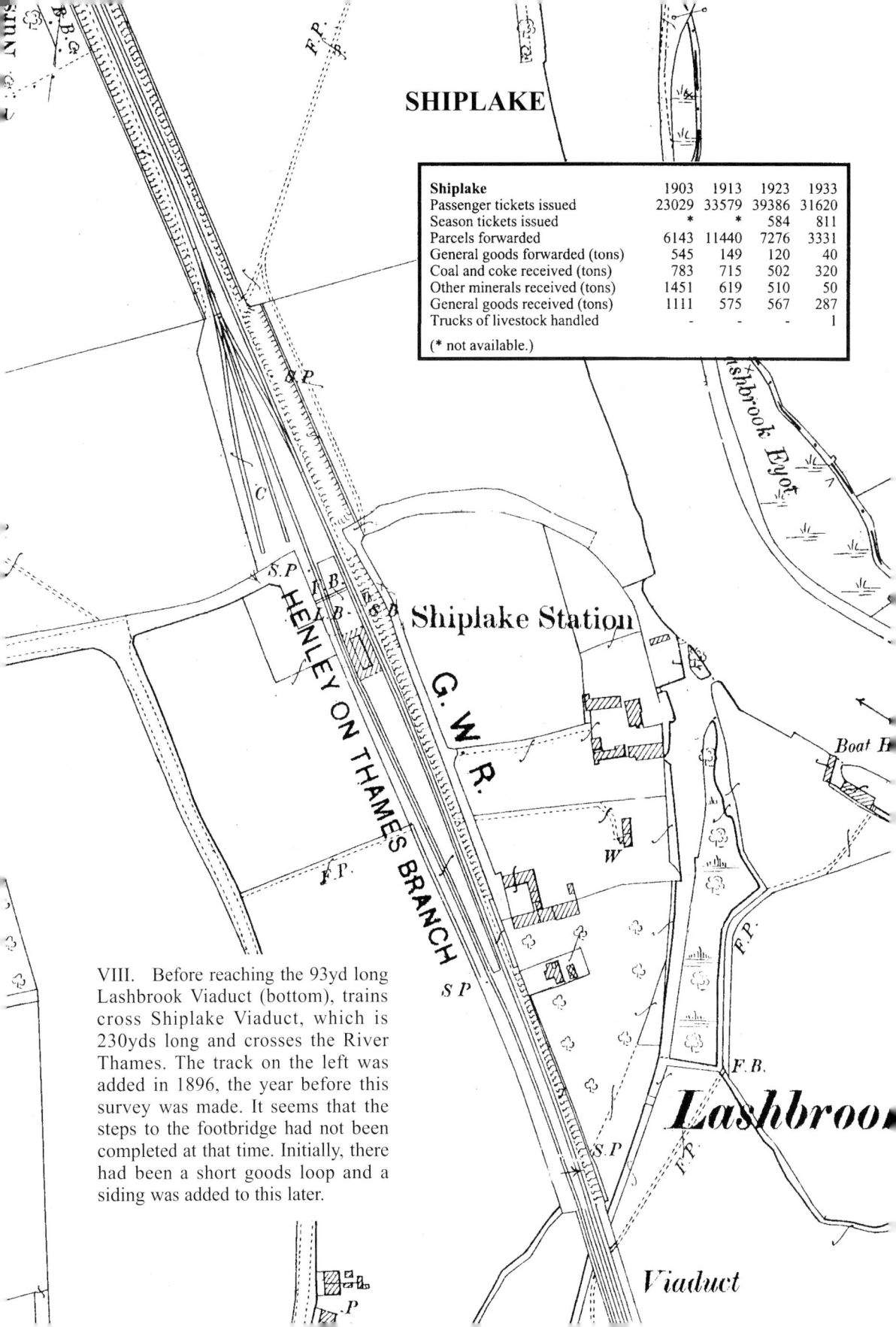

Shiplake	1903	1913	1923	1933
Passenger tickets issued	23029	33579	39386	31620
Season tickets issued	*	*	584	811
Parcels forwarded	6143	11440	7276	3331
General goods forwarded (tons)	545	149	120	40
Coal and coke received (tons)	783	715	502	320
Other minerals received (tons)	1451	619	510	50
General goods received (tons)	1111	575	567	287
Trucks of livestock handled	-	-	-	1

(* not available.)

VIII. Before reaching the 93yd long Lashbrook Viaduct (bottom), trains cross Shiplake Viaduct, which is 230yds long and crosses the River Thames. The track on the left was added in 1896, the year before this survey was made. It seems that the steps to the footbridge had not been completed at that time. Initially, there had been a short goods loop and a siding was added to this later.

17. The station was opened with the line, but its building was destroyed by fire on 26th August 1891. Edwardian-style ladies walk past the new structure and approach the footbridge. The local population rose from 870 in 1901 to 1365 in 1961. (Lens of Sutton)

18. The west elevation is seen in a postcard view, along with the 17-lever signal box which opened on 1st February 1897. Oil lights appear in the previous view - these were superseded by ones using petrol-air gas in 1913. There were five or six men engaged here in the 1930s. (Lens of Sutton)

19. On the platform and near the footbridge is the cream-painted wooden parcels shed. The iron clad shed nearer to us was used for oil lamps and the gas generator. The latter was unreliable and electric lighting followed. The 1893 3½-ton crane was replaced by one of 30cwt capacity a few years later. (Lens of Sutton)

20. As at Wargrave, there was no door on the village side of the building, but here the second track came alongside it. The hut in the distance was for ticket inspectors who were prone to delay down trains substantially. Ticket checking ceased here in 1933. The photo dates from 1919. (LGRP/NRM)

21. The coach was provided for camping purposes in the Summers of 1956-63. Subsequently coal staithes were built from old sleepers on the site of the siding. A loop was created after the branch was singled in 1961, this remaining in use until 11th May 1968.
(Lens of Sutton)

22. The signal box seen in pictures 18 and 19 was replaced by this 22 lever box, which was in use from 14th June 1961 until 20th March 1972. The goods yard closed on 7th September 1964 and the level crossing was fitted with automatic lights in 1973. The white screen obscured the doorway to the gents.
(C.L.Caddy)

23. The buildings were demolished in December 1985 in favour of a mere bus shelter. Fortunately, bushes and trees have grown to reduce the starkness of the wide platform. No. 165003 is bound for Twyford on 22nd October 1997. Seven-coach trains appear on peak-hour Paddington services and on Regatta days.
(F.Hornby)

HENLEY-ON-THAMES

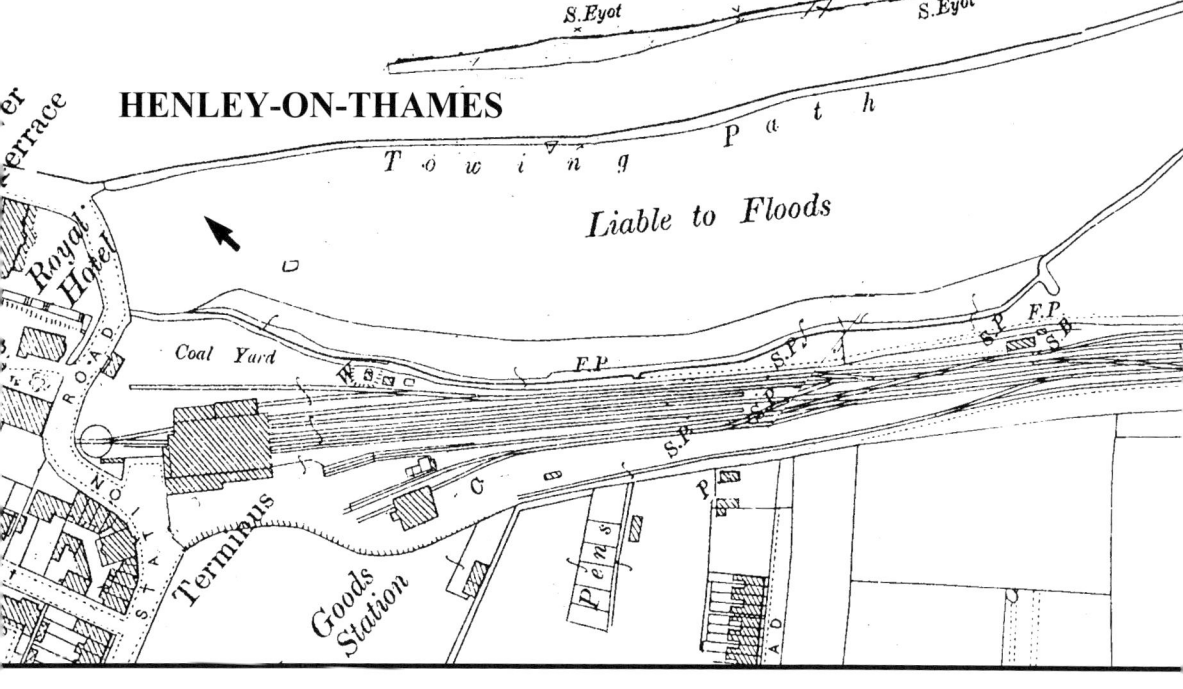

IX. The map shows the layout in 1897 with the 45ft turntable available for engine release. Station Road belonged to the GWR until 1877. Mill Lane signal box (right) was built in 1896 and the level crossing was replaced by a bridge in the following year. The box closed in 1919, it being used mainly during Regatta Week.

24. The suffix -ON-THAMES was not added until 1st January 1895. This postcard was produced soon after, when the road was still unsurfaced and before one of the unusually tall chimneys was blown down. (Lens of Sutton)

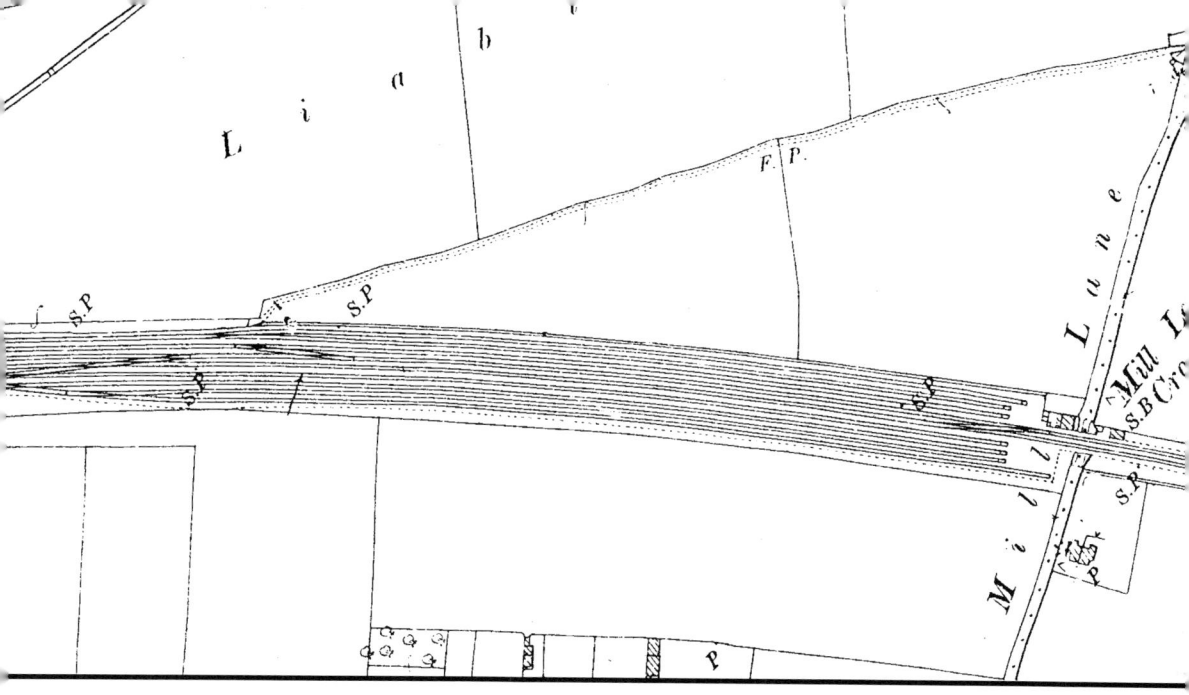

25. The left part of the previous picture was altered in 1904 and a new booking hall was created. Even with a lantern roof, it could not compete with the architecture opposite. The road from here to the bridge over the Thames was not completed until 1862. The gate on the left was for enginemen only. (Lens of Sutton)

Henley-on-Thames	1903	1913	1923	1933
Passenger tickets issued	94789	100784	105076	91238
Season tickets issued	*	*	1421	2303
Parcels forwarded	69988	89368	48074	59186
General goods forwarded (tons)	4296	5190	2596	2431
Coal and coke received (tons)	5653	3932	3519	2295
Other minerals received (tons)	2999	3896	4133	5921
General goods received (tons)	13161	12970	9046	4721
Trucks of livestock handled	264	238	123	37

(* not available.)

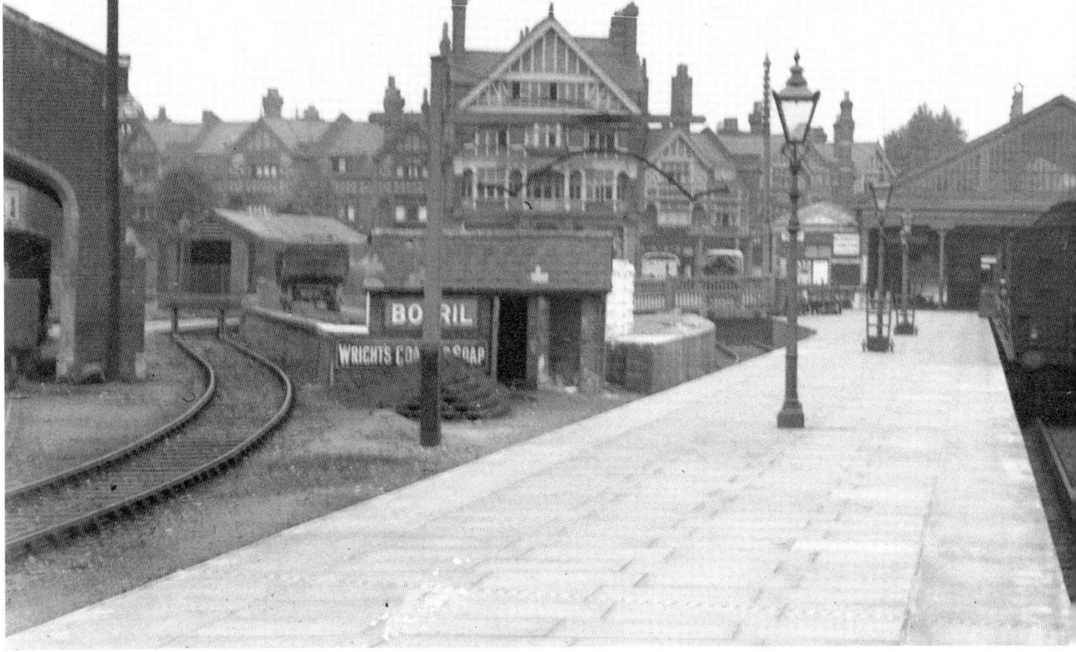
BO RIL
WRIGHTS CO SOAP

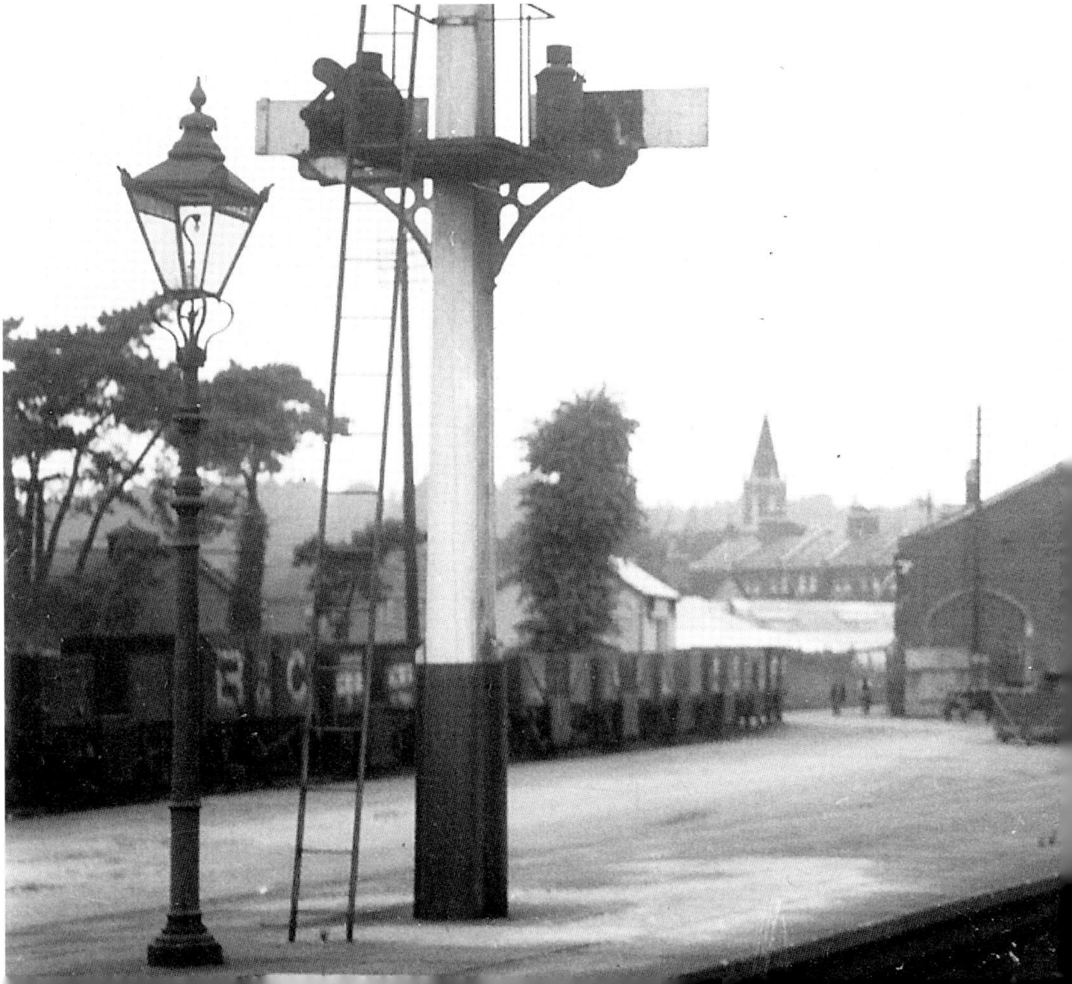
B & C

26. The platforms were numbered 1 to 3 from right to left, but this was reversed soon after nationalisation. The platforms serving the centre track were always both No. 2 and commonly used for arrivals. A 55ft turntable was installed at the end of the curved siding on the right in 1903. This panorama is from 1919. (LGRP/NRM)

27. The platforms were extended greatly in 1891 as the Regatta was increasing in popularity and generating immense traffic. The shunting signals are of the centre pivot type and the gas lamps are Sugg's Windsor pattern. There was a staff of 24 to 27 men between the wars. The goods yard closed on 7th September 1964. (M.Dart coll.)

28. Seen on 18th June 1949 is no. 5932 *Haydon Hall* with a train composed of two 4-car suburban sets and a single nondescript coach next to the engine. This was the largest type that could use the turntable here. An 0-6-0PT stands near the engine shed. (J.H.Meredith)

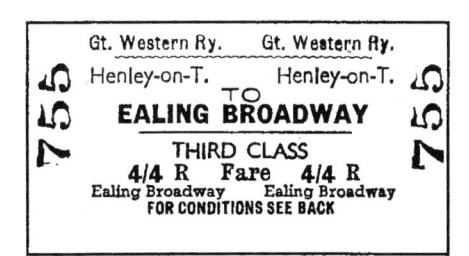

29. One of the 9400 class 0-6-0PTs takes water on 21st April 1957. It was obtained from a well by means of an electric pump. Prior to 1950, a steam pump was housed in the shed on the right and a hose from the branch engine provided the energy. (B.W.Leslie/GWS)

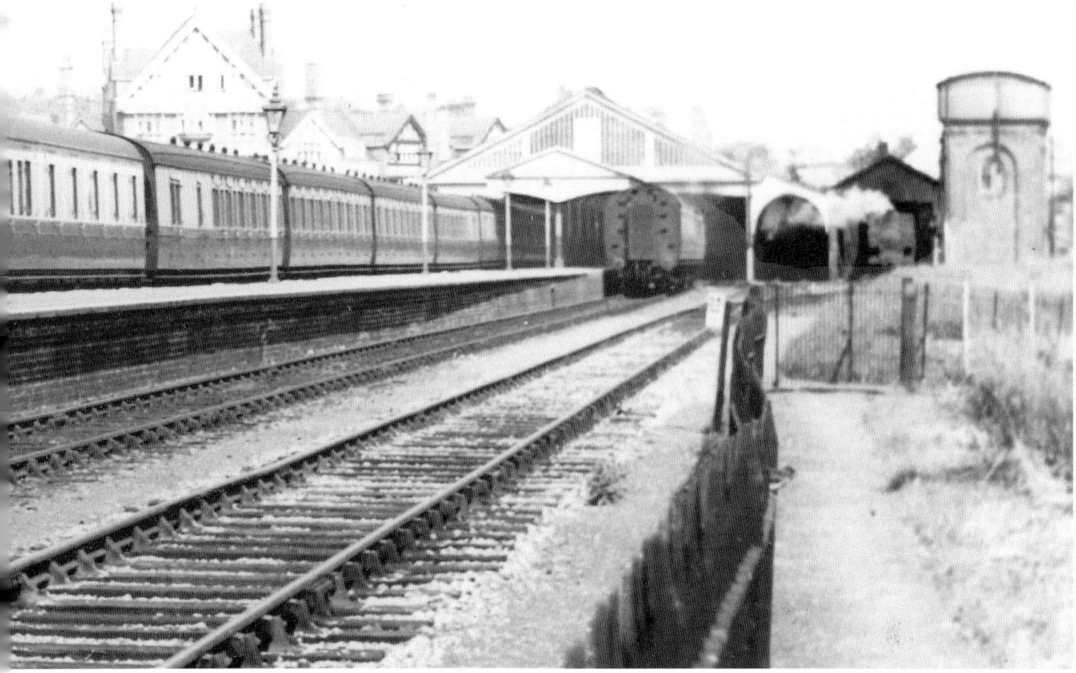

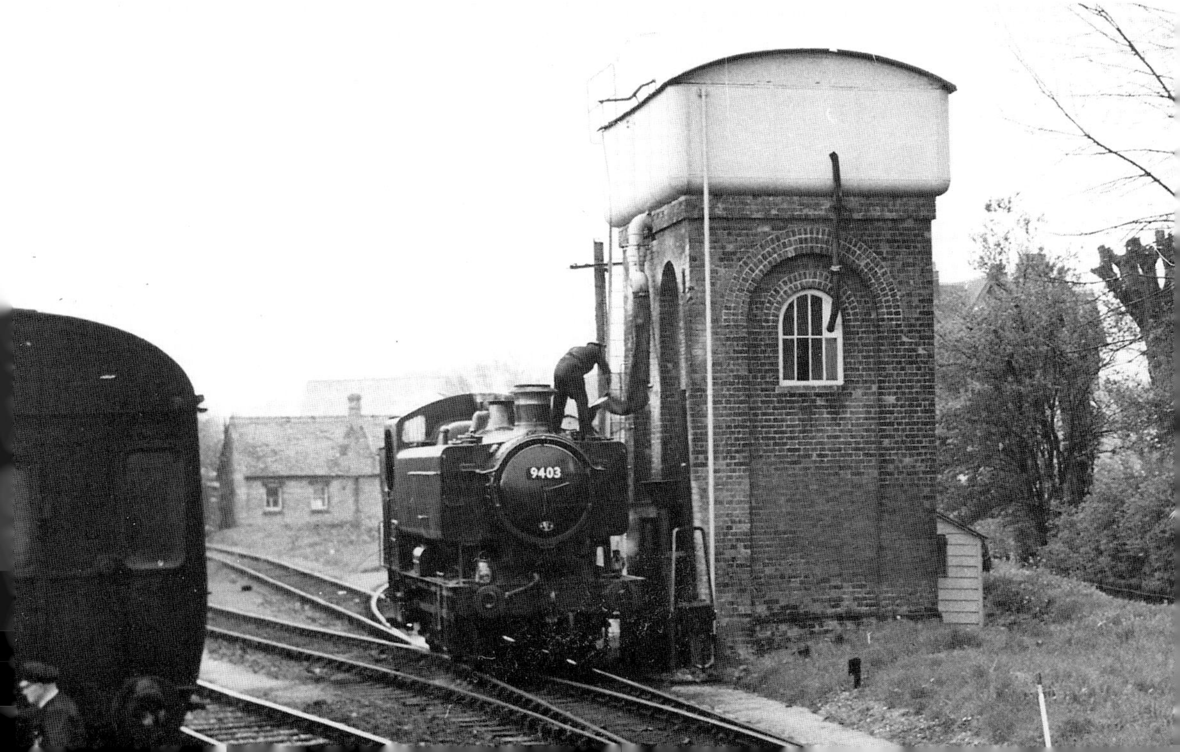
9403

30. A 1954 photograph reveals that the booking hall doors were in line with the platforms. It also shows the smoke troughs and one of their vents on the roof. The cycle shed (left) arrived in 1948. (I.D.Beale)

31. The engine shed closed on 5th October 1958 and local services were operated subsequently by DMUs of this type, although some through trains to Paddington continued to be steam hauled until 14th June 1963. This photograph was taken from the ticket barrier which was erected in 1933. (Lens of Sutton)

32. The platform canopies were erected in 1904, as little more than one coach could stand in the train shed. The space on the right had a line from the turntable until 1903 and subsequently a siding for coach storage. (Lens of Sutton)

33. The 54-lever signal box dated from 1897 and replaced one with a 30-lever frame. Most of the many sidings were removed in 1968-69, but the box continued to be manned until 20th March 1972. Reading Panel then took control of the branch and its two terminal platforms. (C.L.Caddy)

34. This and the previous photograph are from July 1968. The nearest platform was taken out of use on 16th March 1969 and the remaining two were renumbered (3 became 1 again) when the signal box closed. The enamel nameboards date from the mid-1950s. Two camping coaches were in the yard for the 1964 season only. (C.L.Caddy)

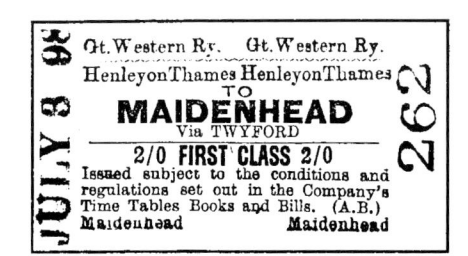

35. Platform 2 lasted until 1986 when the area was levelled for car parking. The original structures were destroyed and a new building (left) was erected. No. 165127 waits to work one of the hourly services to Reading on 10th November 1994. The Thames Turbos represent the third generation of DMUs in the area and were introduced in 1992. (F.Hornby)

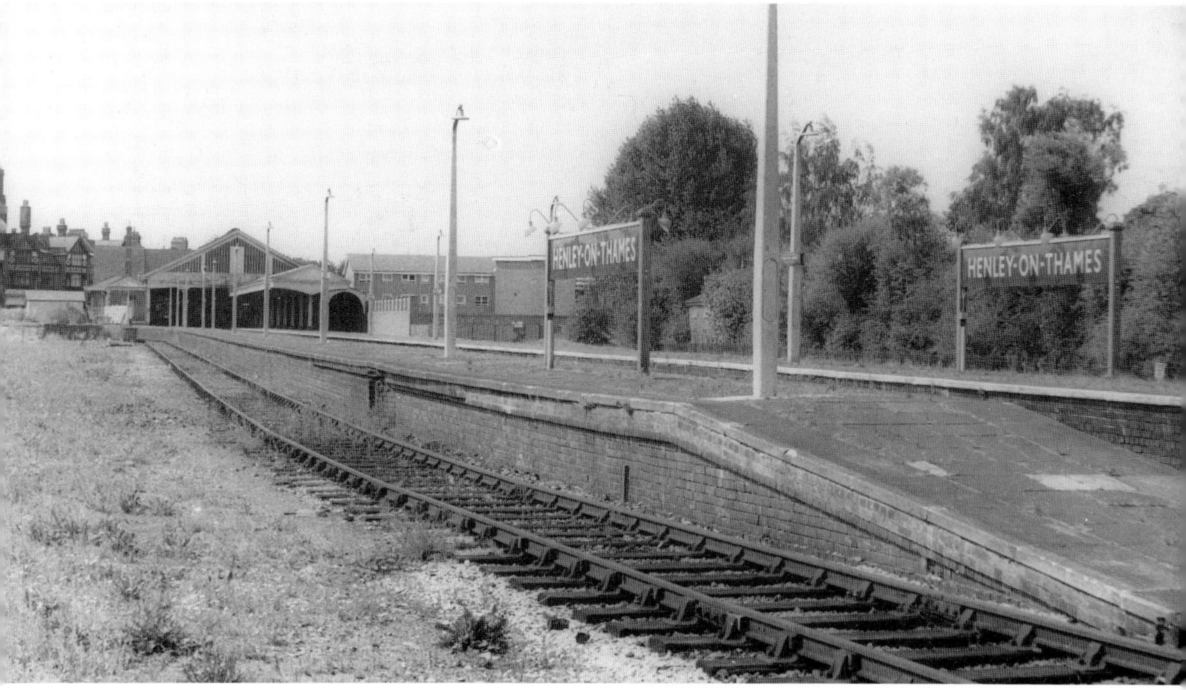
HENLEY-ON-THAMES
HENLEY-ON-THAMES

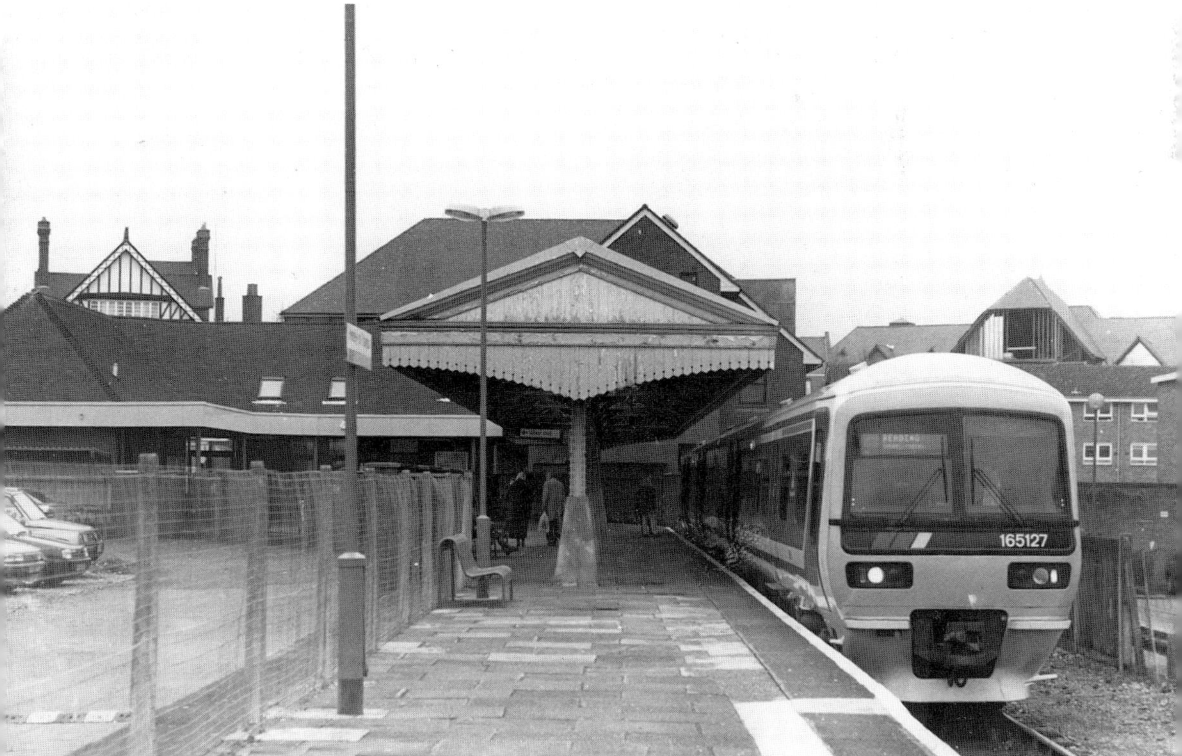
165127

36. The 1904 canopy was retained, but the platform was shortened slightly. The site of the goods yard was transformed to a coach park. A steam shuttle was operated on the first two Sundays of November 1992, with a class 37 at the rear. The 2-6-0 no. 46521 was provided by the Severn Valley Railway. (D.Watts)

37. The new building was completed in 1985 and includes a ticket office which was staffed for most of the day when photographed in 2000. The insetting of the doors creates a pleasing sheltered area. (V.Mitchell)

2. Windsor Branch

X.   The 1945 edition at 1ins to 1 mile features the triangular junction west of Slough station, the entire 2½ mile long branch and part of the SR route through Datchet, which appears in our *Waterloo to Windsor* album.

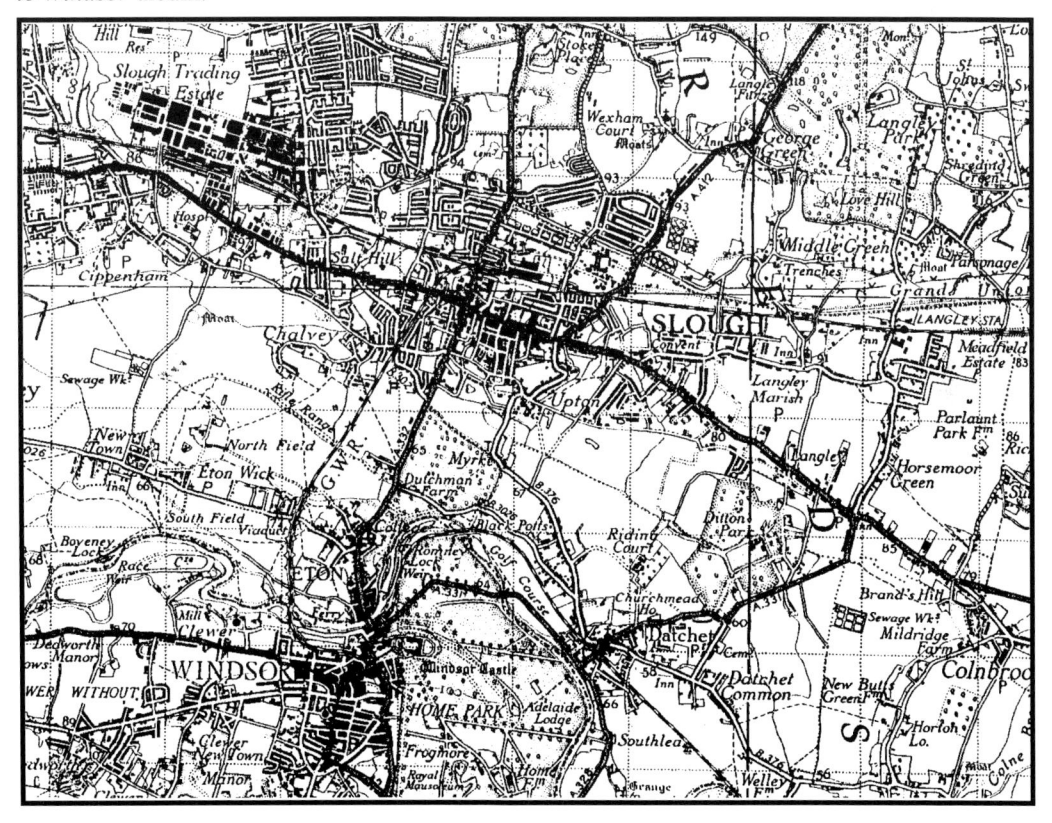

SLOUGH

XI.   Eton College objected to the provision of a station within three miles. Thus trains simply stopped here and passengers had to climb to and from ground level. When one was eventually built, it was in two parts - down on the left and up on the right, the arrangement applying to most other GWR main line stations. The official opening was on 1st June 1840. The plan is from 1879.

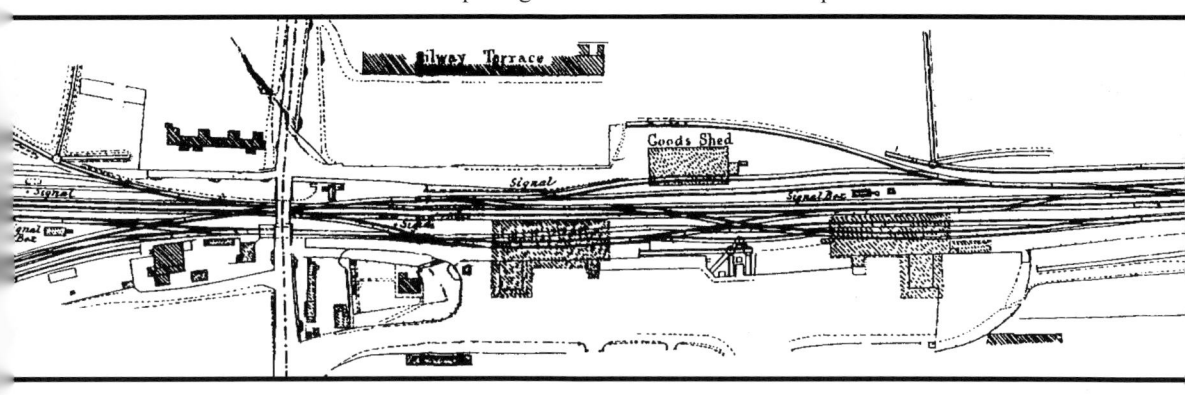

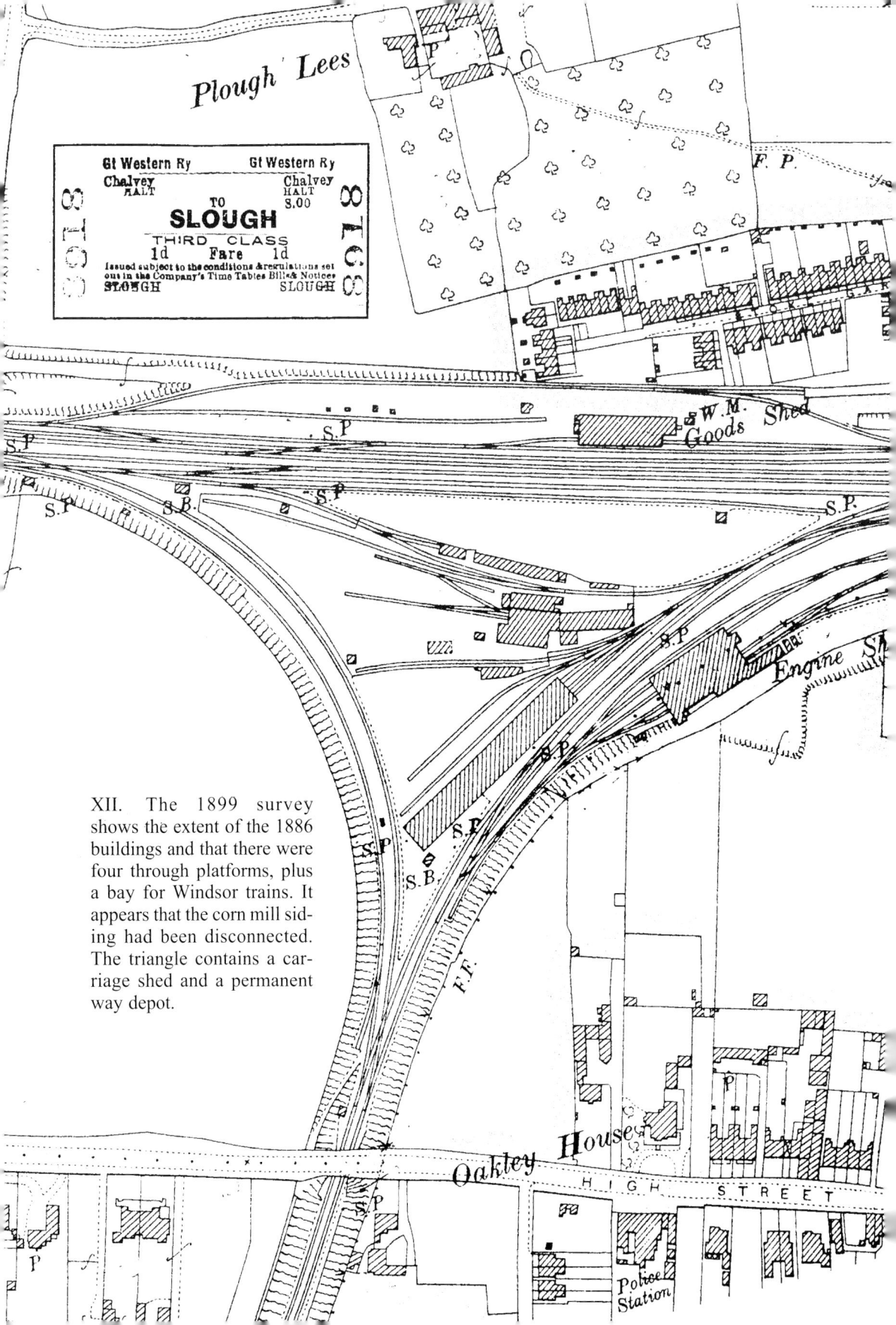

XII. The 1899 survey shows the extent of the 1886 buildings and that there were four through platforms, plus a bay for Windsor trains. It appears that the corn mill siding had been disconnected. The triangle contains a carriage shed and a permanent way depot.

MILL STREET

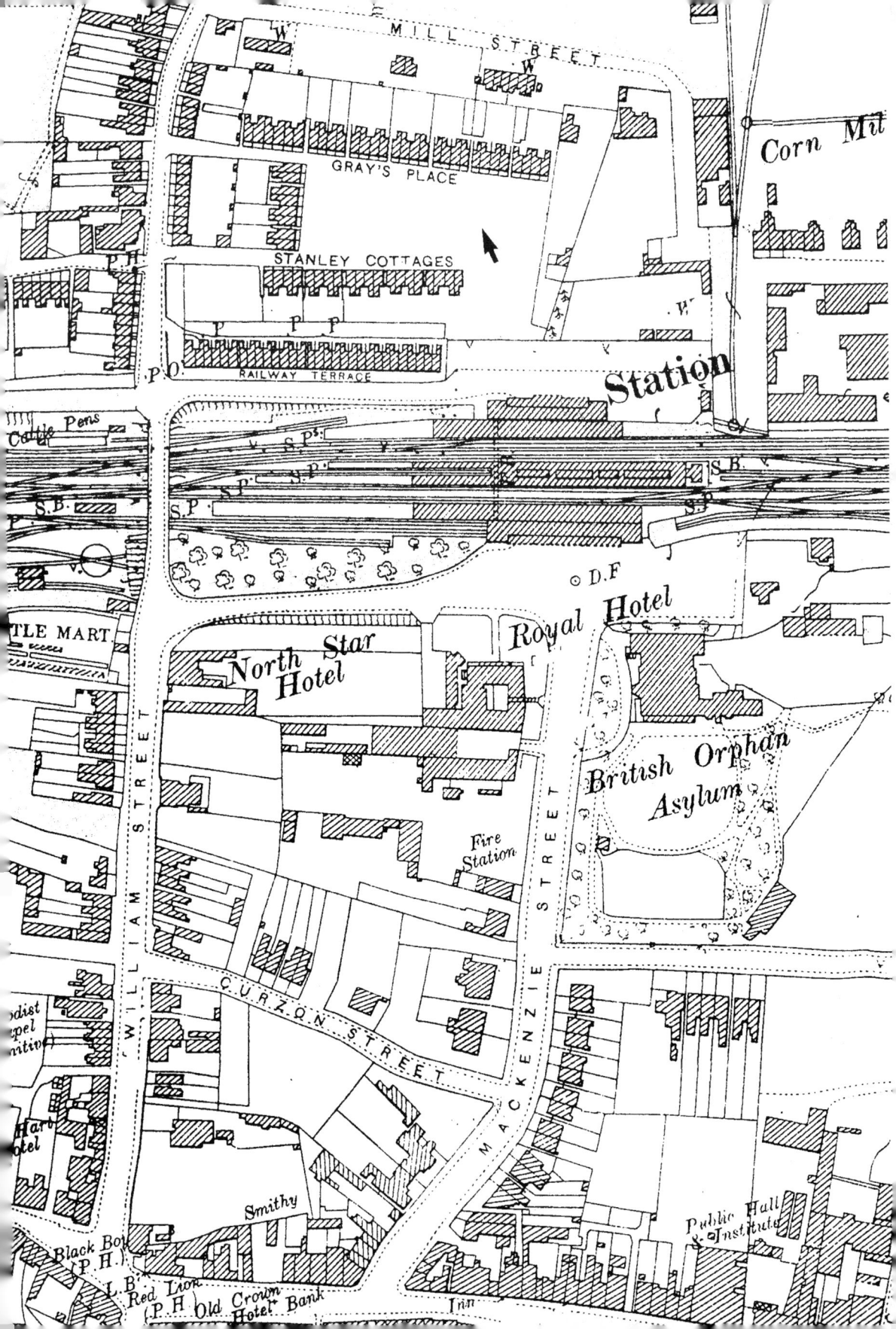

GRAY'S PLACE

STANLEY COTTAGES

Corn Mill

RAILWAY TERRACE

Station

Cattle Pens

TLE MART

North Star Hotel

Royal Hotel

British Orphan Asylum

Fire Station

WILLIAM STREET

MACKENZIE STREET

CURZON STREET

Smithy

Black Boy P.H.

Red Lion P.H.

Old Crown Hotel & Bank

Inn

Public Hall & Institute

38. Looking east in 1919, we see the Windsor Bay on the right and a local train (with milk van) on the left. Also on that side, another bay platform is evident. For many years this was used by trains to and from the Slough Trading Estate. (LGRP/NRM)

> **Other photographs and maps of this station can be found in our *Ealing to Slough* and *Slough to Newbury* albums.**

39. No. 6143 leaves on the down relief line on 23rd February 1958 heading the 2.2pm Paddington to Windsor train. The lorries are a reminder that the GWR established a depot for its Road Motor Engineer on the north side of the running lines. (B.W.Leslie/GWS)

40. The bay had an engine release road until July 1962, although DMUs had started to work most branch services in 1959. Previously some had been operated by GWR diesel railcars and a petrol-electric car had been tried in 1912. Steam railmotors were used between 1913 and 1930, with autocoaches following. (Lens of Sutton)

41. The 11.02 departure to Windsor was recorded on 9th June 1978. Note that the centre bay had been infilled (in 1961) and that the up dock was used for mail traffic. There had been a through line between the two tracks on the left, but it was removed in October 1958. (T.Heavyside)

42. The south facade was recorded in July 2000, its unusually ornate roof being made from metal pressings. The ridges are similar and include rosettes. The pavilion roofs and iron railings are worthy of careful study, although of French style and not from a British railway tradition. (V.Mitchell)

43. A westward panorama from the road bridge includes Middle Box (101 levers and closed on 14th October 1963), the engine shed, the carriage shed and the goods shed. The latter was replaced by a much larger one, seen in the next picture with its doorway occluded by a white panel. The box was superseded by Slough Panel, which was built in the foreground. (LGRP/NRM)

WEST OF SLOUGH

44. Hybrid 2-car DMU set no. L211 (formed of class 101 and a 115 driving trailer) arrives with the 11.57 from Windsor & Eton on 4th April 1990. The newly laid car park on the left is on the site of the former down bay loop and sidings. (G.Gillham)

45. The 13.00 departs for Windsor on 13th April 1994 and will take the left of the two reversible lines that run parallel for nearly ½ mile. The RA is illuminated by platform staff to indicate "Right Away" to the driver. Driver-only operation was authorised on 17th March 1988. (M.Turvey)

46. Moving further west, but back to 1919 again, we look east from the bridge seen in the right distance in the previous picture and see the rest of the goods yard, together with the 1905 West Box. This was replaced in 1930 by one with 95 levers that lasted until 14th October 1963. On the right is West Curve, also known as "Queens Curve", as it was used by Queen Victoria more than passenger

47. The first engine shed had a single track and was replaced in 1868. There were four covered lines by 1872 and the fifth one (left) came in 1935. This undated photograph was probably taken not long before the shed closed in June 1964. (Lens of Sutton)

trains. However, there was a Windsor-Basingstoke and a Windsor-Maidenhead service in some Edwardian years. There were excursion trains also, in later times particularly. It was later considered bad practice to leave wagons on running lines, as seen on the right. The explanation may lie in caption 49. (LGRP/NRM)

48. This is the north end of the shed in May 1962. The office precluded one of the tracks passing out of this end; it was thus used for locomotives receiving attention from the fitters. (T.Wright)

49. Bath Road Junction was at the southern apex of the triangle and in latter years its box was only open for a few hours each morning for freight working. It is seen in 1919, it having opened in 1913 with the GWR's first electro-pneumatic system. Steam was provided from the engine shed to an air compressor working at 70psi. The 20 miniature levers were replaced by 23 conventional ones in 1931. West Curve was singled on 9th September 1963 and eliminated on 25th July 1970. A wagon appears to be derailed. (LGRP/NRM)

SOUTH OF SLOUGH

50. Four local roads converge at this bridge and Chalvey Halt was opened adjacent to it on 6th May 1929 to draw traffic from these highways. However, results were poor and closure followed on 6th July 1930. This and the next photograph were taken on 10th October 2001. (T.Wright)

XIII. About 450 yds south of the halt, a siding was provided for the Slough & Datchet Electric Light Company. It was in use from 14th June 1912 until 27th January 1952 and is seen on the 1934 map.

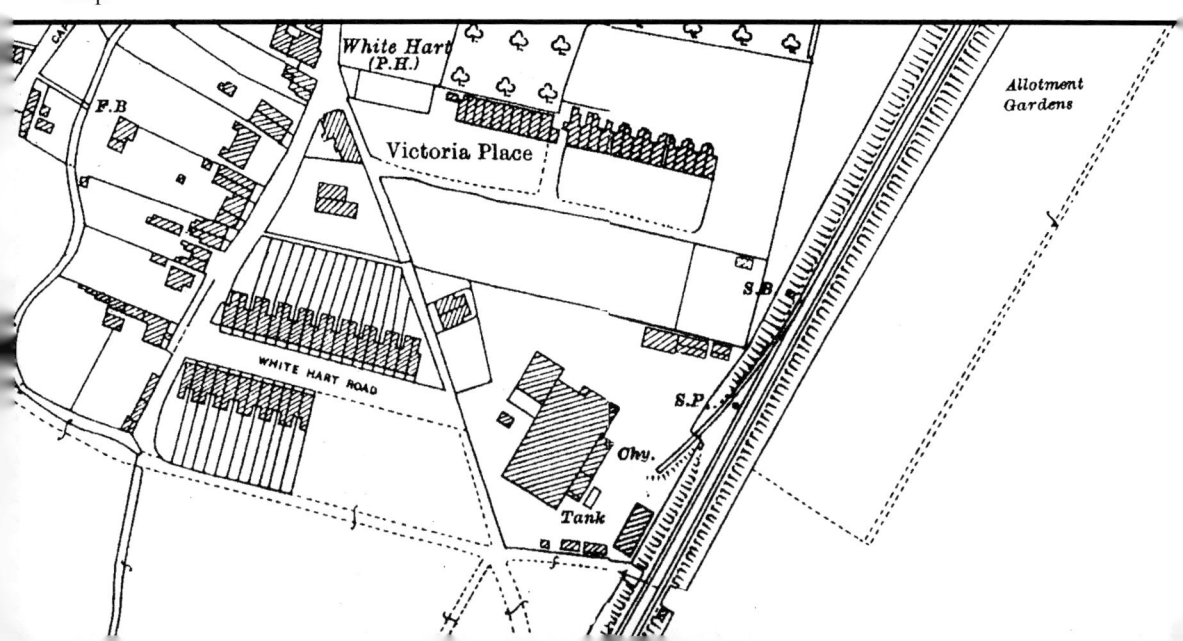

51. No. 165129 runs between two modern structures - the M4 overbridge and the bridge over the flood relief channel. The waterway has been given the name Jubilee River. This northward view is from the new A332 dual carriageway, which also required a fresh bridge over the branch. (T.Wright)

NORTH OF WINDSOR

52. Almost one mile of the route was constructed on viaduct across the flood plain of the Thames Valley. The original timber structure was replaced mainly by brick arches. The DMU is on Folly Bridge, a steel span over Eton Wick Road, on 16th July 1983. Eton signal box opened on 4th June 1889, but was used only occasionally until closed in 1939. (T.Wright)

53. The bridge over the Thames was substantially rebuilt in 1907 - even the abutments were replaced, although the original girders were retained. It was photographed in 1993, when it was subject to a 35mph speed limit. (T.Wright)

54. Perfect peace: a former sleeping car retired to a redundant barge and was pictured near Windsor in July 1967. (T.Wright)

55. Another steel span was provided over this popular backwater. Boats can be seen on the mainstream under the centre of no. 55024 as it exposes a tower of Windsor Castle. It is bound for Slough on 2nd August 1990. (T.Wright)

56. Some of the many arches are evident as a gleaming Thames Turbo rounds the curve into the station on 14th June 1993. It is working the 10.18 from Paddington, the first through train from London for many years. (T.Wright)

WINDSOR & ETON CENTRAL

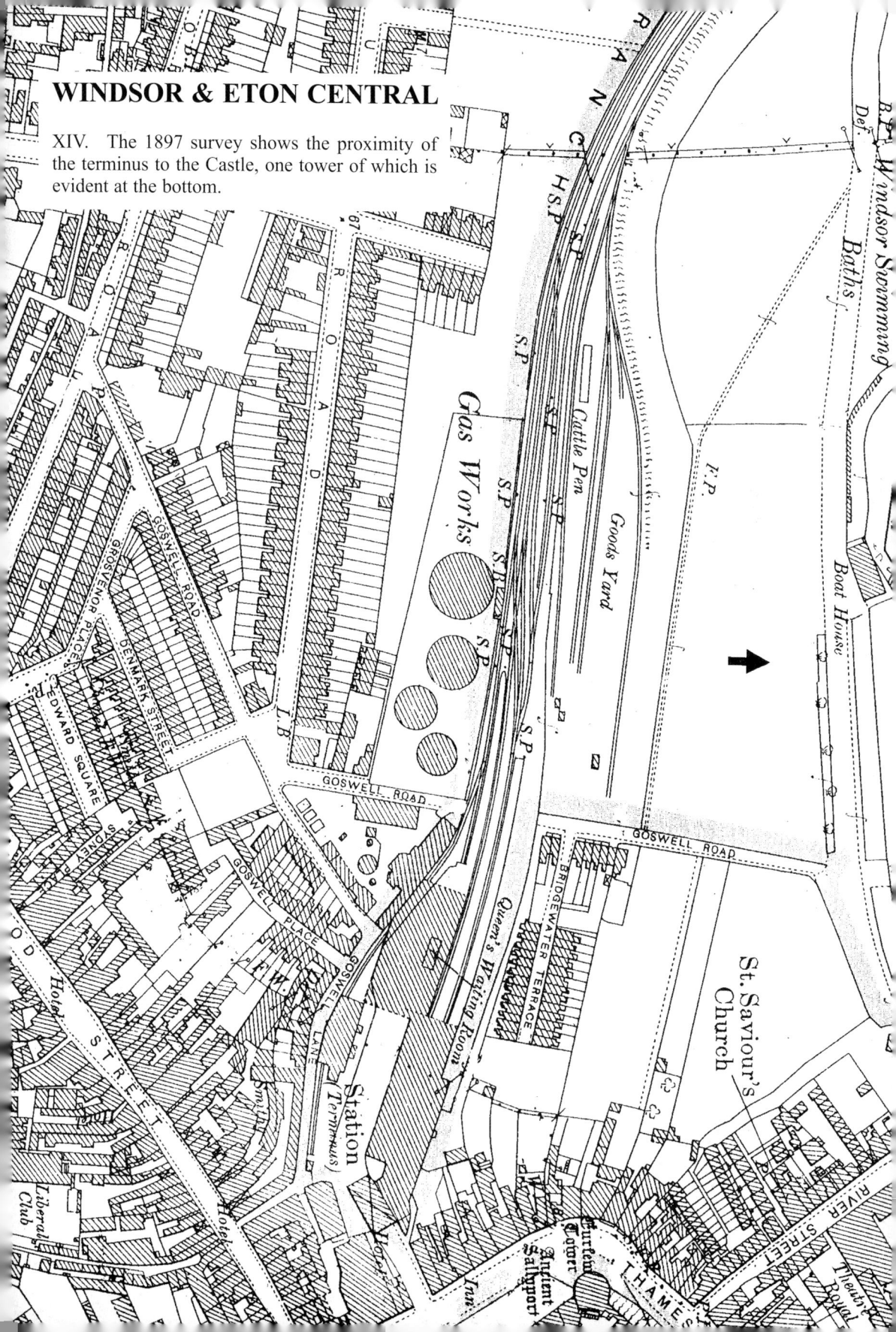

XIV. The 1897 survey shows the proximity of the terminus to the Castle, one tower of which is evident at the bottom.

57. The first station had a train shed, as at most GWR termini. It is illustrated after the introduction of mixed gauge in 1862. The branch was noted for having trains composed of different gauge stock, one vehicle having couplings offset at one end. Three goods sidings were later provided on the right and a berthing siding was laid in the middle of the shed after the elimination of broad gauge here in 1883. (British Railways)

58. In recognition of Queen Victoria's diamond jubilee in 1897, the GWR rebuilt the station on a grand scale with lavish facilities. Note that there were even booking offices for different classes of passengers in that class conscious era. (Lens of Sutton)

Windsor and Eton	1903	1913	1923	1933
Passenger tickets issued	228766	186247	311933	97751
Season tickets issued	*	1402	3291	2804
Parcels forwarded	120189	143803	66503	89136
General goods forwarded (tons)	3472	3982	1472	704
Coal and coke received (tons)	5033	2108	1652	2710
Other minerals received (tons)	5398	5482	4340	4083
General goods received (tons)	14269	15263	8344	4795
Trucks of livestock handled	156	189	32	14

(* not available.)

59. After leaving the spacious concourse, travellers could use the CLOAK ROOM (centre), a euphemism for left luggage and not toilets. They would then use the covered carriageway, the other end of which is seen in the next picture. (Lens of Sutton)

PLATFORM Nº 3
PLATFORM Nº 2
PLATFORM Nº 1
1ST & 2ND CLASS BOOKING OFFICE
STATION MASTER'S OFFICE
3RD CLASS WAITING ROO

CLOAK ROOM

60. Those leaving on foot would pass under the Jubilee Arch and experience a rising gradient to the Castle, which is behind the camera. While the footway is paved, the roadway is unsurfaced. Although tarmacadam had not arrived, setts of granite or hardwood could have been used. The suffix & ETON was added on 1st June 1904. (British Railways)

61. The train is standing at platform 4 in 1919. The line on the right served the goods shed, which is shown parallel to Goswell Lane on the map. The low level goods yard, west of the station, had been created during the 1895-97 alterations. (LGRP/NRM)

62. No. 5409 is sandwiched between two autocoaches and is departing for Slough from platform 2. The perforated signals controlled shunting movements. The staff numbered about 50 in the 1900s, 40 in the 1930s and 30 in the 1950s. There was one clerk only in 2000. (Lens of Sutton)

63. Railcar no. W30W is also leaving platform 2, but after CENTRAL had been added to the name on 26th September 1949. The wagons are on the goods siding, which had a hopper that allowed direct discharge of coal into the gasworks, part of which was located under the arches. (N.Simmons)

64. The RCTS "Berks & Wilts Tour" stands at platform 4 on 9th April 1961. The platform canopies had been extended in 1908. More of the goods line is evident in this view. (F.Hornby)

65. The engine release crossover is evident in this picture of platforms 1 and 2 taken on 24th August 1963. In the background is the roof seen in picture 58. The branch was singled on 9th September 1963. (T.Wright)

66. The signal box (centre) replaced one that was on the other side of the tracks on 5th May 1963. It lasted until 17th November 1968, when it was moved to Viaduct Junction, Kensington. The inclined wall to the left of it is adjacent to the line that descends at 1 in 45 to the goods yard. This closed on 6th January 1964, but had handled only coal in its final six weeks. (M.Dart coll.)

67. Set no. 414 leaves platform 2 in May 1969, not long before its closure. The gasworks was in use from 1827 to 1951, coal consumption examples being 9250 tons in 1900 rising to 13,900 tons in 1948. One arch of the viaduct housed a GWR compressed oil gas holder, the gas being made at Wormwood Scrubs. (T.Wright)

68. The carriage road was used as a bus terminal for over 80yrs. An Alder Valley Leyland National is in front of a Bristol VR bound for Camberley on 23rd January 1975. (T.Wright)

69. Madam Tussaud's took a lease on most of the station area and opened an exhibition called "Royalty and Railways" on 1st April 1983. Many were fooled by Dean 4-2-2 no. 3041 *The Queen*, which had been created at Carnforth using only a few genuine components. The upper half of each driving wheel does not exist, but steam was made to issue from appropriate parts. (M.Turvey)

70. Coach no. 229 is also a replica and placed in it were wax figures of Queen Victoria's eldest daughter (Empress Frederic of Prussia) and her son (Prince Henry). On the left is the chairman of the GWR and in black is the Windsor stationmaster. The other coach was no. 233, a genuine former royal train vehicle that had served as a holiday home at Aberporth for about 50 years. (T.Wright)

71. The royal waiting room had last been used as such in 1936 and became the area HQ for British Transport Police in November 1950, finally being used by a newspaper wholesaler until 1963. The figures represent Queen Victoria (right) and the Prince and Princess of Wales. Only a ladies toilet was provided - the new King soon had that rectified. The exhibition was renamed "Royalty and Empire" to improve its appeal. (T.Wright)

72. Platforms 3 and 4 were taken out of use on 17th November 1968 and no. 2 followed on 5th September 1969. No. 1 was drastically shortened on 22nd November 1981 and is seen in July 1993 when Network SouthEast livery was in use. (T.Wright)

73. The splendid exhibition was abandoned by its new owners in 1991 and further buildings encroached on the remaining platform. The RA sign and associated emergency red signal were not in use when no. 165003 was photographed on 16th October 2001. To the right of the railings and under the curved glass is a walkway serving the coach park in the former goods yard. (T.Wright)

74. The fine booking hall from 1897 was restored to form the entrance to the exhibition. It has subsequently served as an enquiry office for all occupants of the commercial complex, but train times are not available. (T.Wright)

75. The spectacular canopy was provided purely for ceremonial occasions and was of little value to passengers. Under it is the Bath stone royal waiting room, unloved and unlabelled, simply forming side rooms to the Ha! Ha! Bar. (V.Mitchell)

76. The *Queen* has been deprived of her tender (ex-SECR) and her impressive coaches, her steelwork showing rust in 2001. Clearly King Cash ruled in this domain. Train tickets were available from a tiny shop to the right of the departure indicator on the right. (V.Mitchell)

3. Maidenhead to High Wycombe

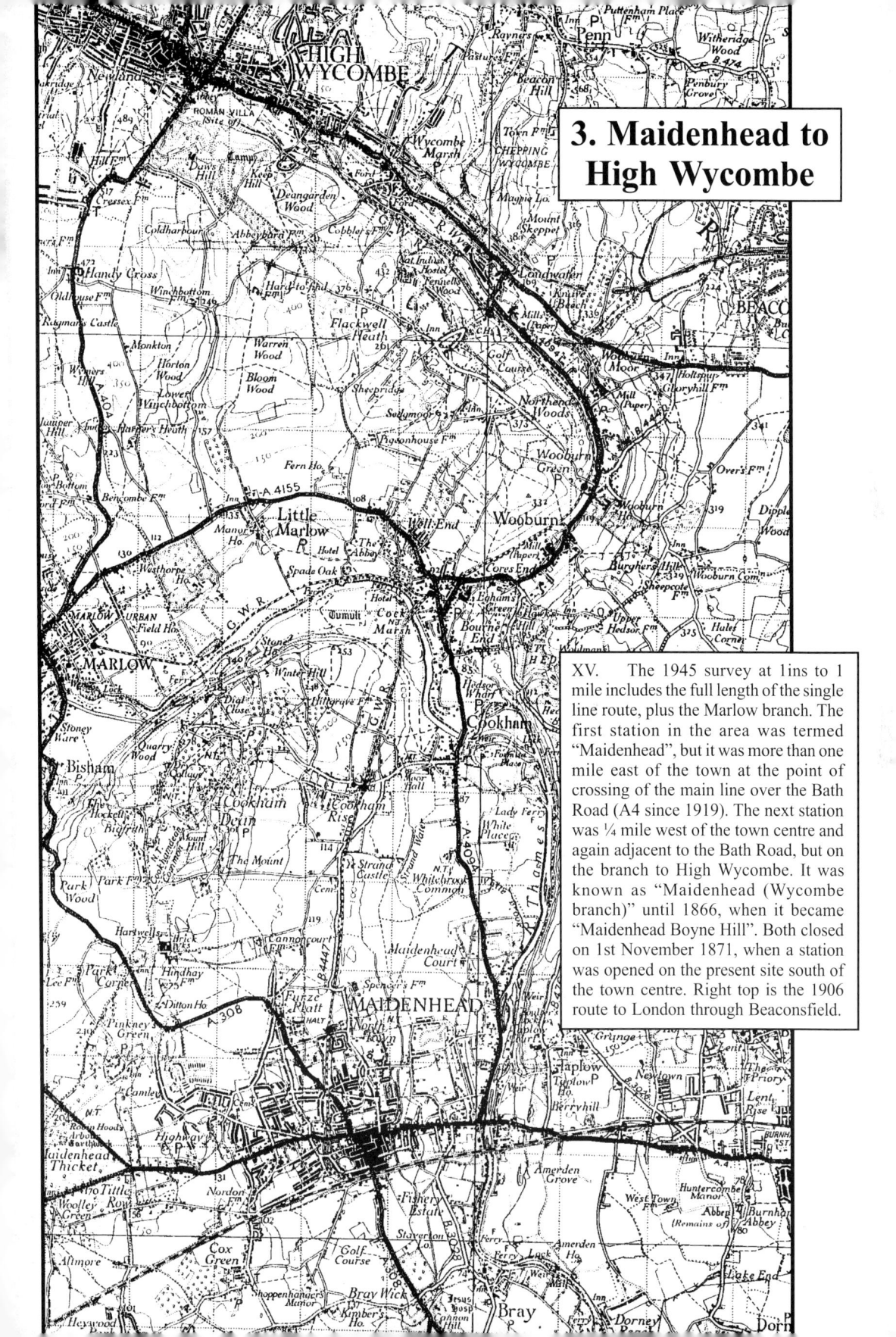

XV. The 1945 survey at 1ins to 1 mile includes the full length of the single line route, plus the Marlow branch. The first station in the area was termed "Maidenhead", but it was more than one mile east of the town at the point of crossing of the main line over the Bath Road (A4 since 1919). The next station was ¼ mile west of the town centre and again adjacent to the Bath Road, but on the branch to High Wycombe. It was known as "Maidenhead (Wycombe branch)" until 1866, when it became "Maidenhead Boyne Hill". Both closed on 1st November 1871, when a station was opened on the present site south of the town centre. Right top is the 1906 route to London through Beaconsfield.

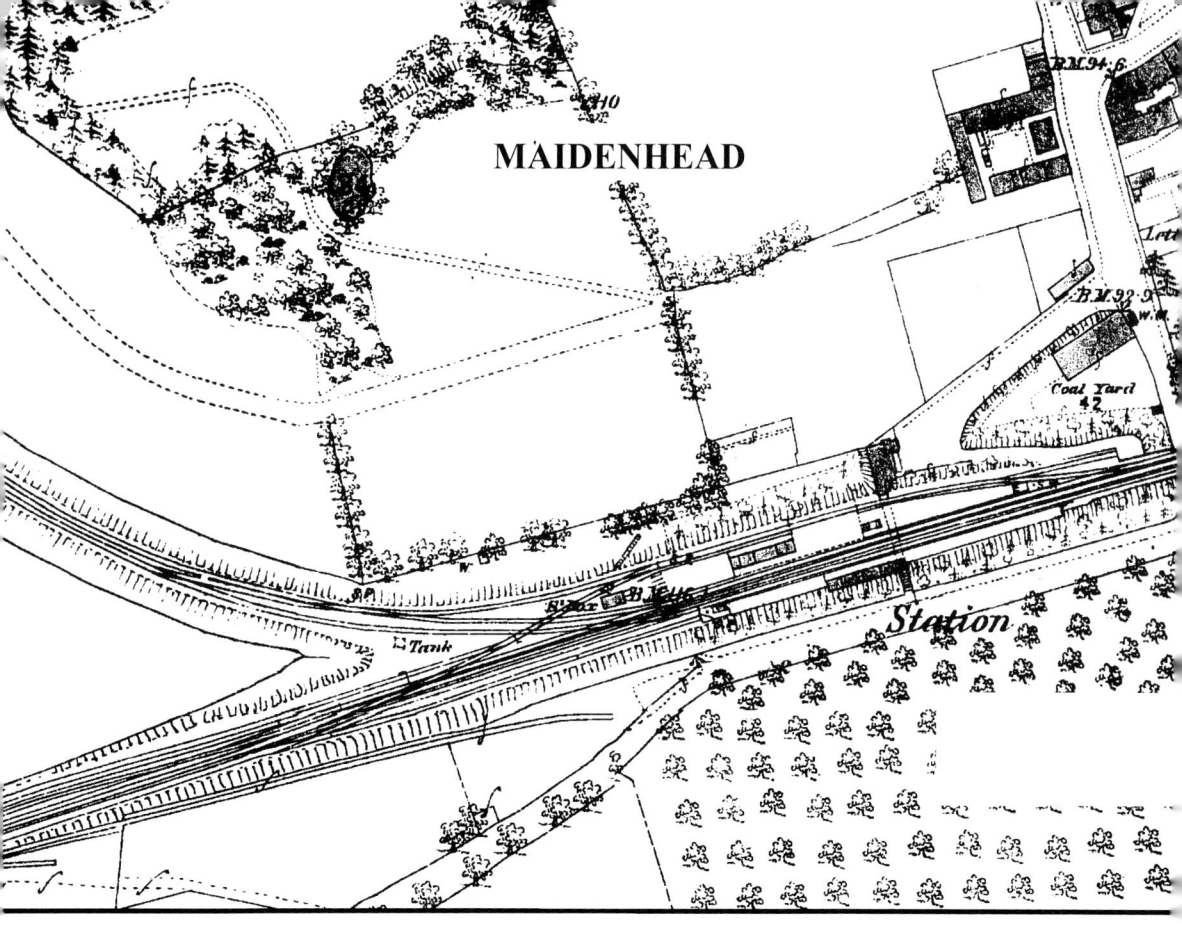

XVI. The 1887 map shows that there were two sidings north of the double track west of the station and two at a low level south thereof.

77. New buildings were erected in 1891 on the platforms, those on the right dating from 1871-72. Their canopy was extended over the advertisement signs in 1923. (British Railways)

78.   A "Metro" class 2-4-0T waits with a branch train, as luggage is loaded into a London-bound train. The booking office is on the right. There were 68 to 74 employed here in the 1930s. (British Railways)

79.   The branch is on the right and coaches stand on a siding formed when the point of convergence to single track was moved nearer to the station in the 1920s. On the left is the goods shed and Middle Box, both dating from 1891, although there was a goods yard here much earlier. (British Railways)

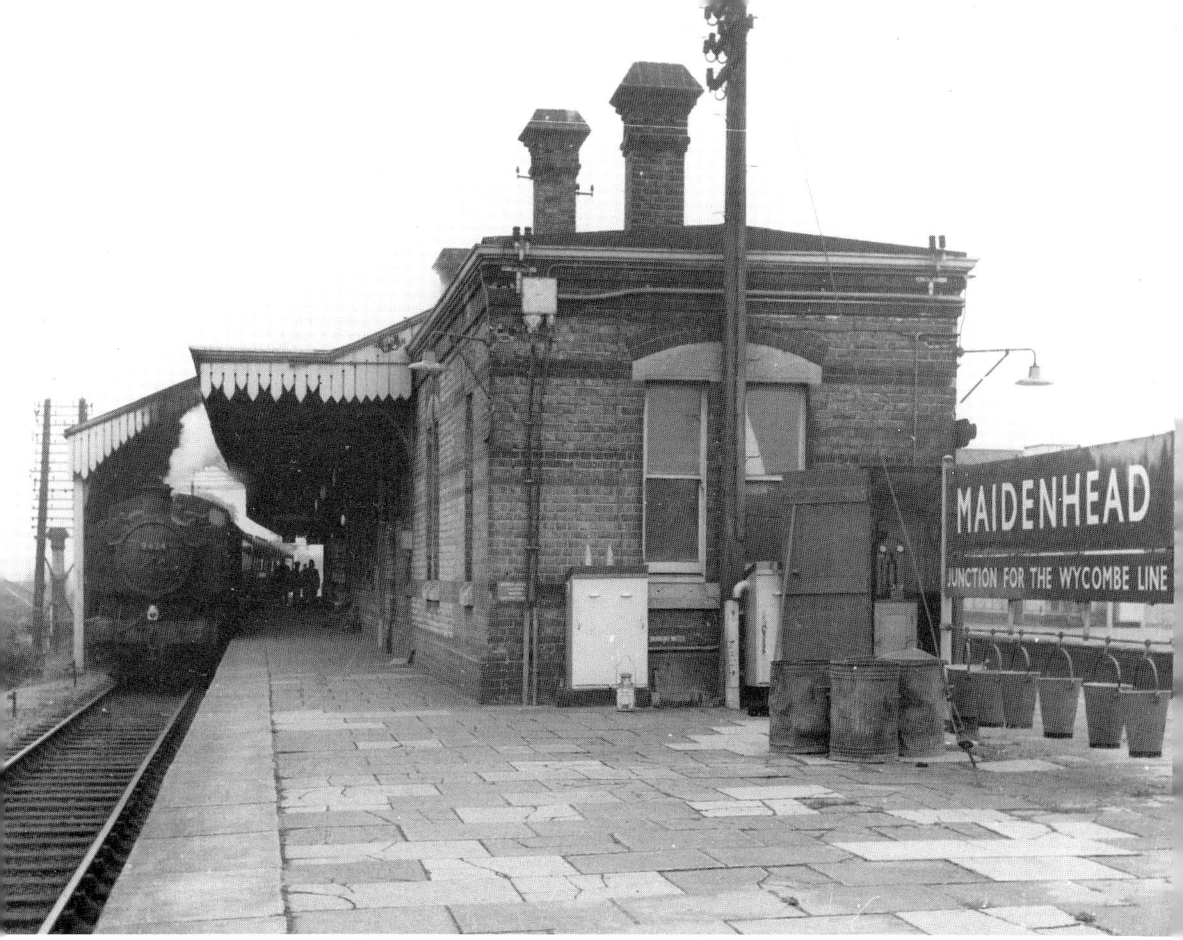
MAIDENHEAD
JUNCTION FOR THE WYCOMBE LINE

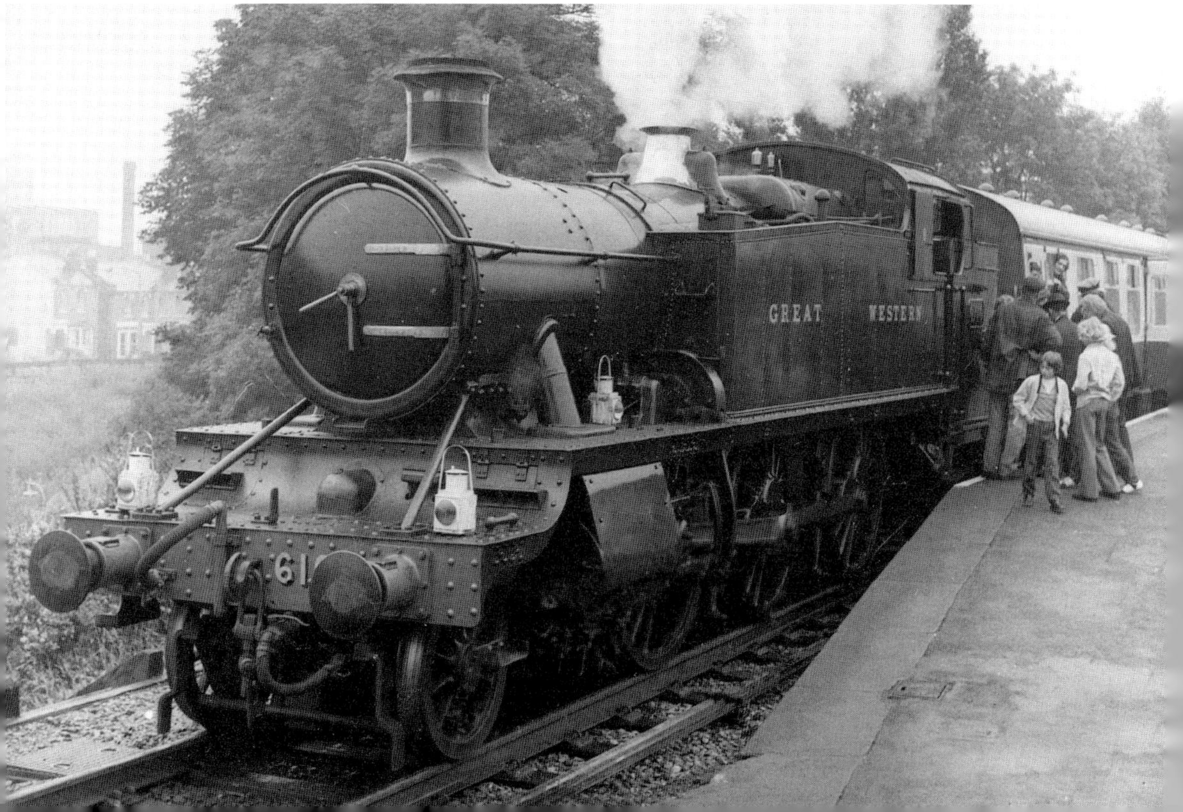
GREAT WESTERN
61

80. The branch train shed was erected in 1871, the loop line being provided from the outset. The single line token apparatus is in the cupboard by the rubbish bins and 0-6-0PT no. 9424 is about to depart for High Wycombe. (Lens of Sutton)

Other pictures of this area are shown in nos 25 to 38 in our *Slough to Newbury* album.

81. No. 6106 was present on 15th July 1973 in connection with the Marlow branch centenary. This 2-6-2T pulled the train to Bourne End and another locomotive was on the other end to draw it back - see picture no. 90. (T.Wright)

82. Improvements in 1913 included provision of a separate luggage subway and associated lifts, together with a substantial extension of the canopy eastwards. Branch services were operated by DMUs of this type from 8th July 1962; this example was recorded on 1st March 1979. (F.Hornby)

83. Thames Turbos were introduced in 1992-93 and brought new levels of comfort. No. 166215 is on the loop line on 13th April 1994, having left Marlow at 12.10. The 15mph speed limit eases to 25 further along the curve. The second track was removed on 21st October 1974. (M.Turvey)

84. The goods yard closed on 19th July 1965, but one of two sidings retained was used for unloading Ford cars. The two were still to be seen on 27th July 2000 as a class 47 brought its train unusually on the up relief line. The three signal boxes were replaced by one on the site in the foreground on 8th December 1963. It had 46 levers and lasted until 21st October 1974. (V.Mitchell)

FURZE PLATT

85. A halt was opened here on 5th July 1937 to serve the village and the developing residential area of North Town. Staff was provided until 1st November 1942 and tickets were issued at the signal box later. This is in the distance in this southward view. (Lens of Sutton coll.)

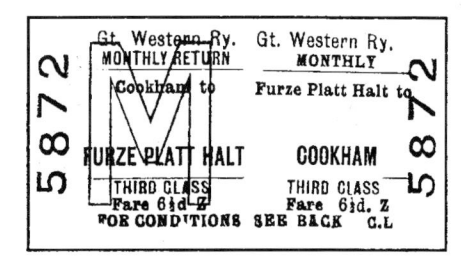

86. The original timber platform was replaced by concrete components, it accommodating five coaches when photographed on 16th October 2001 with no. 165002 present. (T.Wright)

87. No. 165005 is running north in deep shadow on 2nd November 2001. The ticket office was staffed on weekday mornings at that time. (V.Mitchell)

COOKHAM

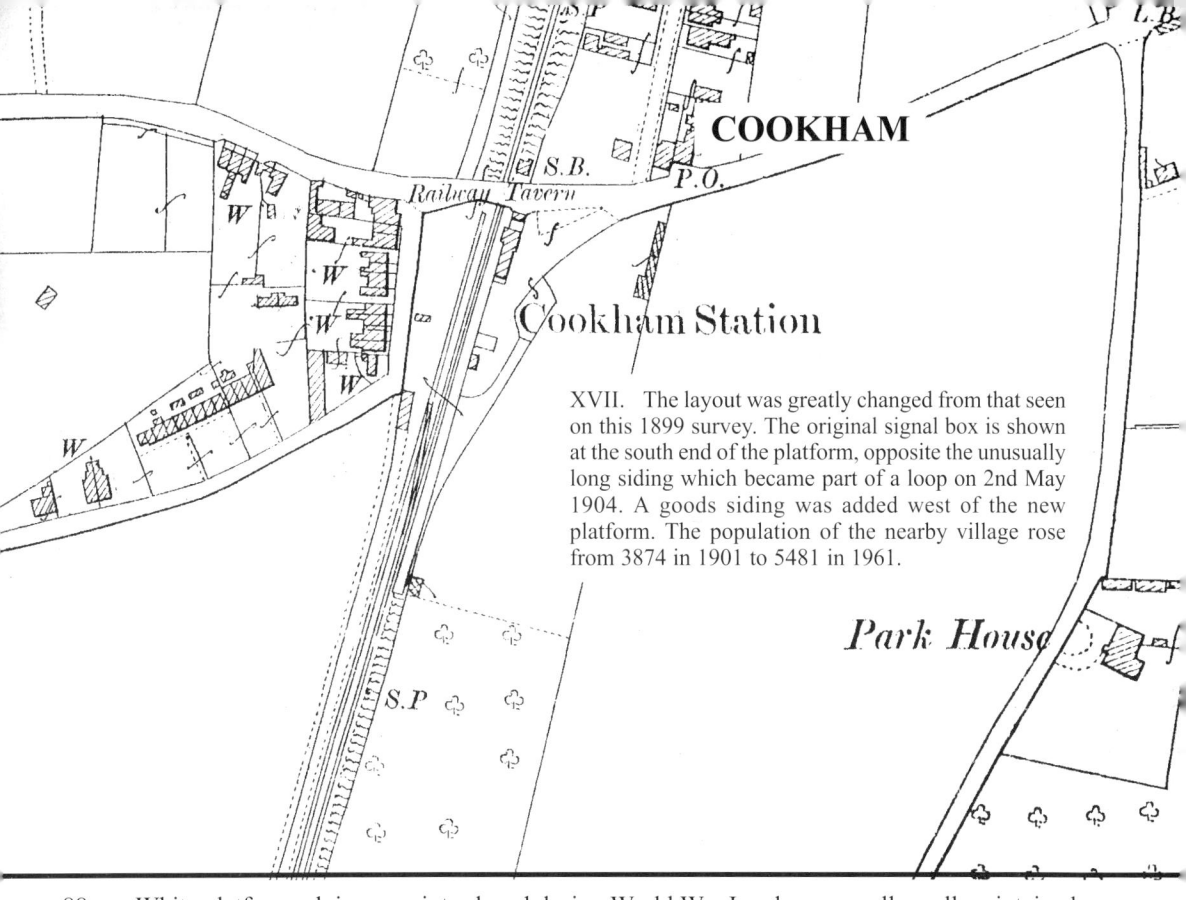

XVII. The layout was greatly changed from that seen on this 1899 survey. The original signal box is shown at the south end of the platform, opposite the unusually long siding which became part of a loop on 2nd May 1904. A goods siding was added west of the new platform. The population of the nearby village rose from 3874 in 1901 to 5481 in 1961.

88. White platform edging was introduced during World War I and was usually well maintained subsequently. This northward view includes the signal box, which had a gate wheel and 18 levers. The footbridge was moved to Pewsey in 1969 and one flight of steps can still be seen on the wrong side of the structure for that location. There were usually 10 to 12 men employed here prior to WWII. (LGRP/NRM)

89. The Wycombe Railway often used flint from the Chiltern chalk and local red brick quoins for their buildings. Railcar no. W14W is working a London Railway Society excursion on 26th September 1954. It largely obscures the signal box which simply controlled the crossing after the singling on 11th May 1969 until closure on 30th September 1973, when half-barriers came into use. (F.Hornby)

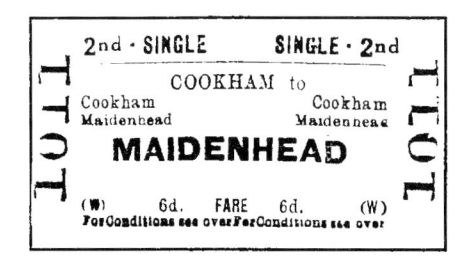

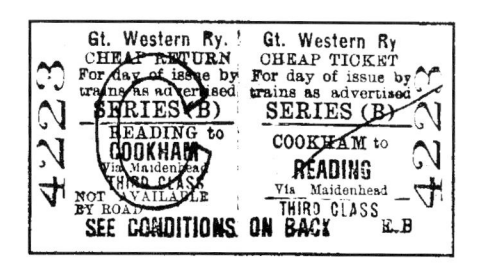

90. No. 6998 *Burton Agnes Hall* of 1949 came from the Didcot Railway Centre to participate in the Marlow branch centenary celebrations on 15th July 1973. The ventilator on the hip roof and the wooden screen below were part of the provision for gentlemen. The semaphore signals would vanish within weeks. (T.Wright)

91. No. 165135 arrives from Marlow on 10th September 1997, the station still being staffed part-time. The building on the down side had been adapted and extended for commercial purposes, the nearby goods yard having closed on 1st March 1965. (F.Hornby)

BOURNE END

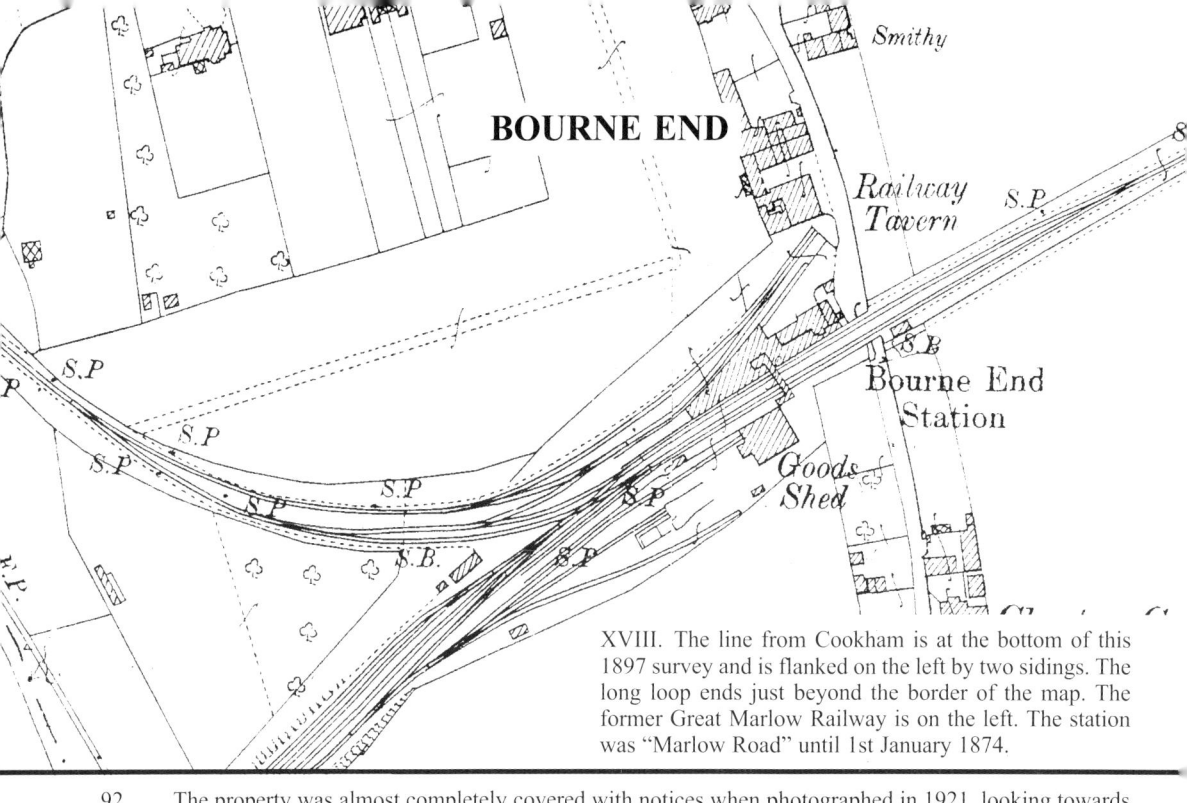

XVIII. The line from Cookham is at the bottom of this 1897 survey and is flanked on the left by two sidings. The long loop ends just beyond the border of the map. The former Great Marlow Railway is on the left. The station was "Marlow Road" until 1st January 1874.

92.   The property was almost completely covered with notices when photographed in 1921, looking towards Maidenhead. Some antique coaches form the Marlow train in the bay and the goods shed stands on the left. About 200yds beyond the signal box is Bourne End viaduct, 162yds in length over the River Thames and beyond it is the 44yd Cockmarsh Common Viaduct. A staff of 21 was required throughout the 1930s. (LGRP/NRM)

93. An unusual occurrence was recorded on 30th July 1949, when 0-4-2T no. 1442 propelled a horse box onto the back of a train to High Wycombe while attached to autocoach no. W201. The line in the centre was added in 1935. (J.H.Meredith)

94. A 1951 photograph features the branch junction and includes the bay line and its parallel loop for running round. The foot crossings were for use by signalmen when conveying tokens and staffs for single line working. (A.J.Pike/F.Hornby)

95. A train from High Wycombe arrives behind no. 6135 on 16th July 1955. The goods shed and associated yard were in use until 11th September 1967. The large poster was offering a cheap day ticket to Paddington for 5/9. (E.Wilmshurst)

96. The branch bay was recorded on 18th February 1958, when 0-4-2T no. 1450 was in charge. This 1935 locomotive now resides on the Gloucestershire & Warwickshire Railway. The run-round loop had been taken out of use on 11th December 1955 and subsequently removed. A train is arriving from Maidenhead in the background. (H.C.Casserley)

Bourne End	1903	1913	1923	1933
Passenger tickets issued	69791	68811	74074	47790
Season tickets issued	*	419	808	1509
Parcels forwarded	23520	32061	23216	19206
General goods forwarded (tons)	5545	5852	5228	5480
Coal and coke received (tons)	9107	4826	739	620
Other minerals received (tons)	3219	2701	2625	3808
General goods received (tons)	8788	9510	10551	9915
Trucks of livestock handled	43	22	38	4

(* not available.)

97. A DMU departs for High Wycombe in the Summer of 1967 and will soon pass over Cores End level crossing, its box being visible in the distance. The route beyond it was closed completely on 4th May 1970, but the section between the level crossings remained in use until 13th June 1971, when North Box was closed. It had 44 levers. (T.Wright)

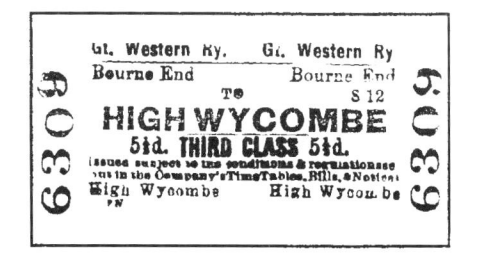

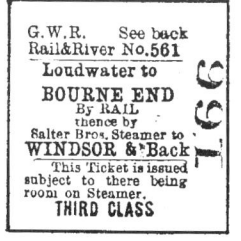

98.   South Box (55 levers) had ceased to function on 30th January 1956. Two trains pass its site: on the left is one from Maidenhead and a Marlow service creeps round the curve on 5th August 1971. A camping coach was stationed here for the Summer of 1960 only. (T.Wright)

99.   The Marlow branch centenary events brought no. 1450 back to its former workplace on 15th July 1973. Two autocoaches were obtained to recreate old times. The traditional "Marlow Donkey" had returned. (T.Wright)

100. The last of the sidings was removed in 1971, but the lines to both former through platforms were retained, the point being controlled by Slough Panel. The staff member has the wooden staff for the Marlow branch in his hand and is approaching the ground frame. He will unlock it and set the branch points himself. (F.Hornby)

101. No. 165001 is bound for Marlow on 6th January 2001, the Victorian single line system still being used. Electric train tokens were used to Maidenhead, a system introduced here in January 1914 and the first on the GWR. Both platforms are used in peak hours, one train operating a connecting shuttle service to Marlow. The historic buildings were intact and staffed in the mornings. (M.Turvey)

Wooburn Green	1903	1913	1923	1933
Passenger tickets issued	44548	40215	47215	17191
Season tickets issued	*	124	302	287
Parcels forwarded	11862	9979	5303	5542
General goods forwarded (tons)	1323	753	904	770
Coal and coke received (tons)	234	442	408	96
Other minerals received (tons)	1273	225	3283	690
General goods received (tons)	3804	3058	3043	2198
Trucks of livestock handled	97	62	52	10

(* not available.)

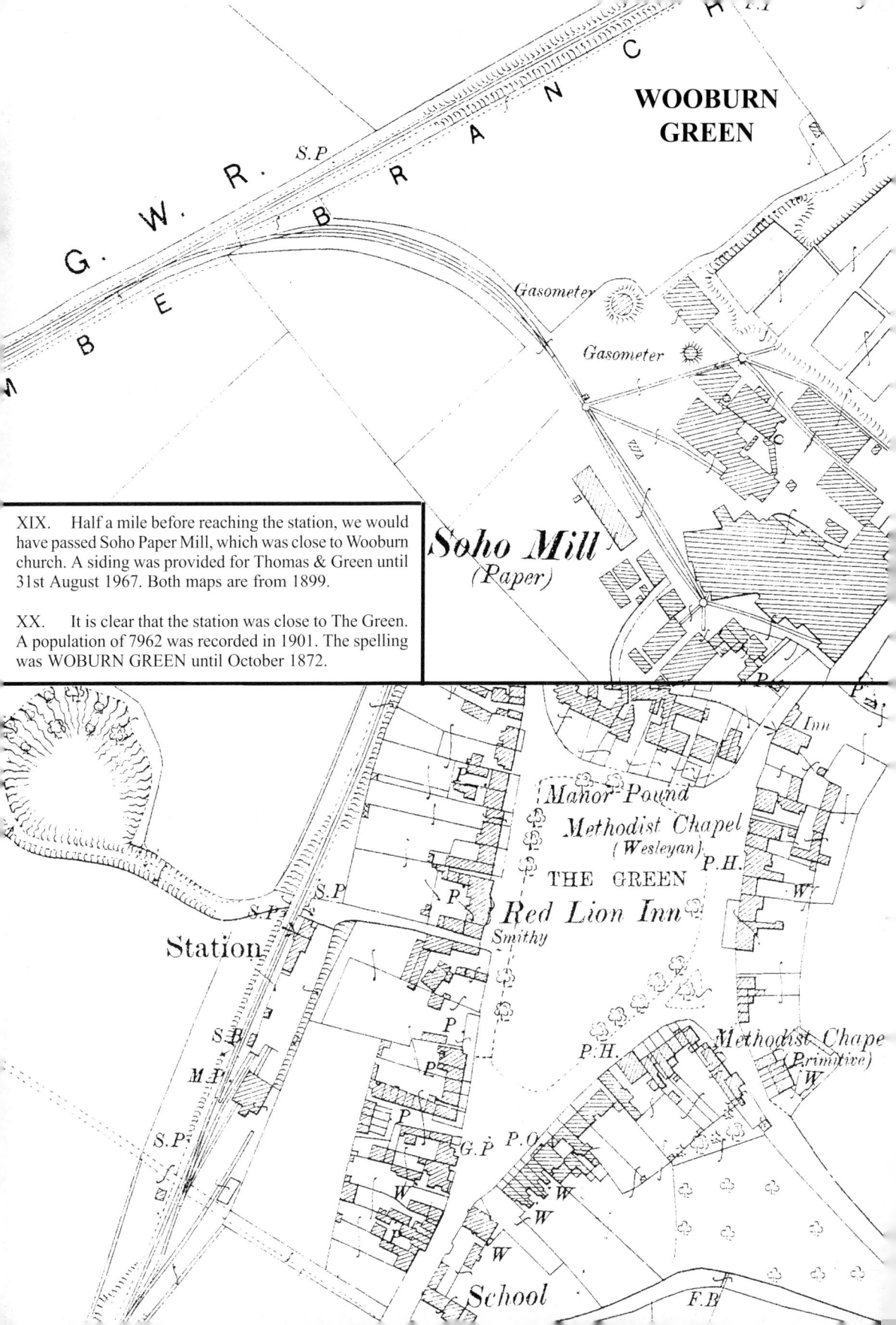

XIX. Half a mile before reaching the station, we would have passed Soho Paper Mill, which was close to Wooburn church. A siding was provided for Thomas & Green until 31st August 1967. Both maps are from 1899.

XX. It is clear that the station was close to The Green. A population of 7962 was recorded in 1901. The spelling was WOBURN GREEN until October 1872.

102. A 1921 southward view includes the goods shed roof behind the signal box and the paper mill chimney beyond the right tablet catcher. Goods traffic ceased on 11th September 1967. There were eight men here in the 1930s, but staffing was only part-time after January 1966. (LGRP/NRM)

103. The signal box was a block post, had 18 levers and remained in use until route closure. No. 122 is bound for Bourne End on 27th September 1969. The only rod remaining is for the gate lock, but all the signals were still in use. (E.Wilmshurst)

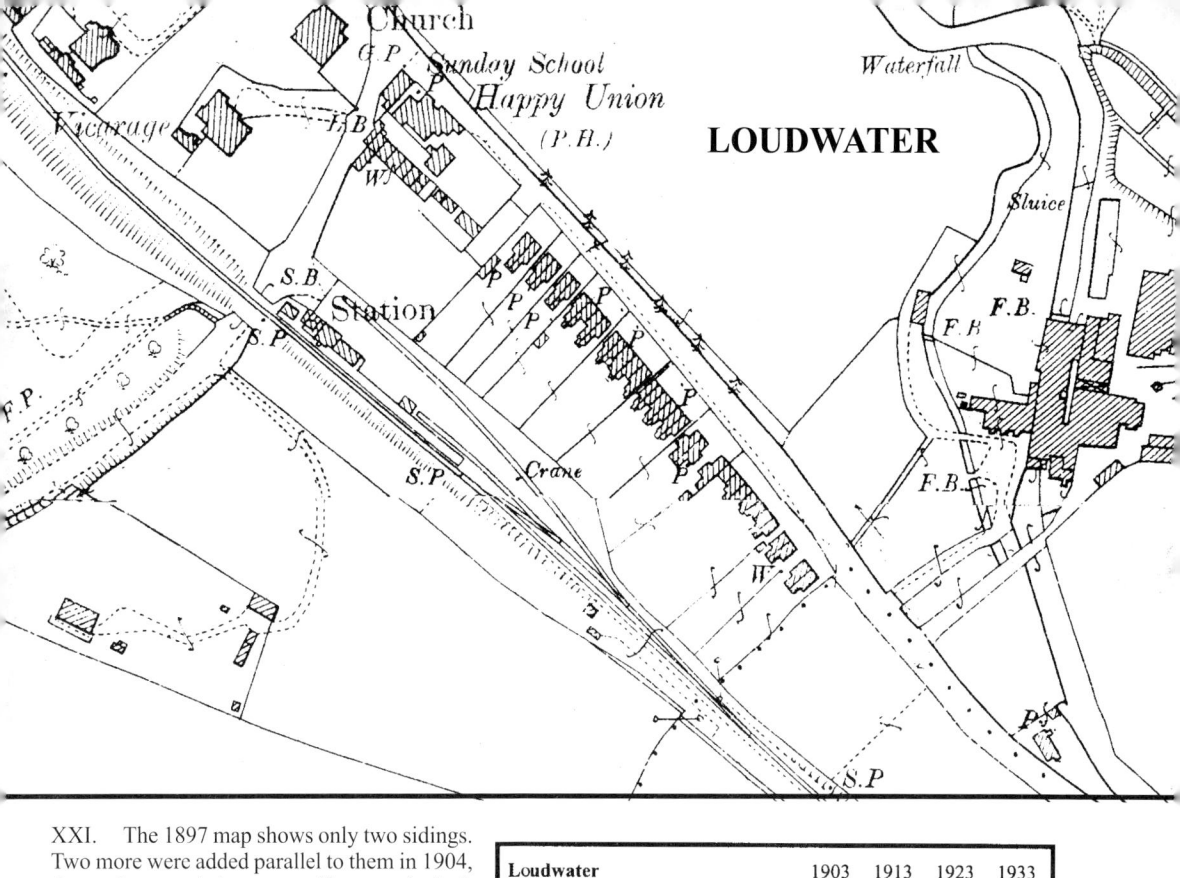

XXI. The 1897 map shows only two sidings. Two more were added parallel to them in 1904, the northern one being spanned by a goods shed. Many of the cottage gardens were thus shortened. On the right is Snakely Paper Mill.

104. The loop line, left on this 1921 picture, was laid in 1904, but it could only be used for passing goods trains. Ten men were engaged here in the 1920s. The goods shed is visible through the railings. (LGRP/NRM)

Loudwater	1903	1913	1923	1933
Passenger tickets issued	51960	60696	82903	26737
Season tickets issued	*	*	426	99
Parcels forwarded	6051	7694	3942	7046
General goods forwarded (tons)	4388	9847	3811	1205
Coal and coke received (tons)	2362	2451	2690	8201
Other minerals received (tons)	2948	2620	3691	819
General goods received (tons)	5380	13620	8179	7990
Trucks of livestock handled	-	-	1	8

(* not available.)

105. This 1921 panorama includes several chimneys of paper mills. The wagons and traffic figures indicate that they required much coal. The early use of water power and later use of electricity may explain the peak. Ford's blotting paper was once a well known local product. A second platform was brought into use on 15th May 1942 and the ring was then taken off the signal arm. The crane was of six tons capacity. (LGRP/NRM)

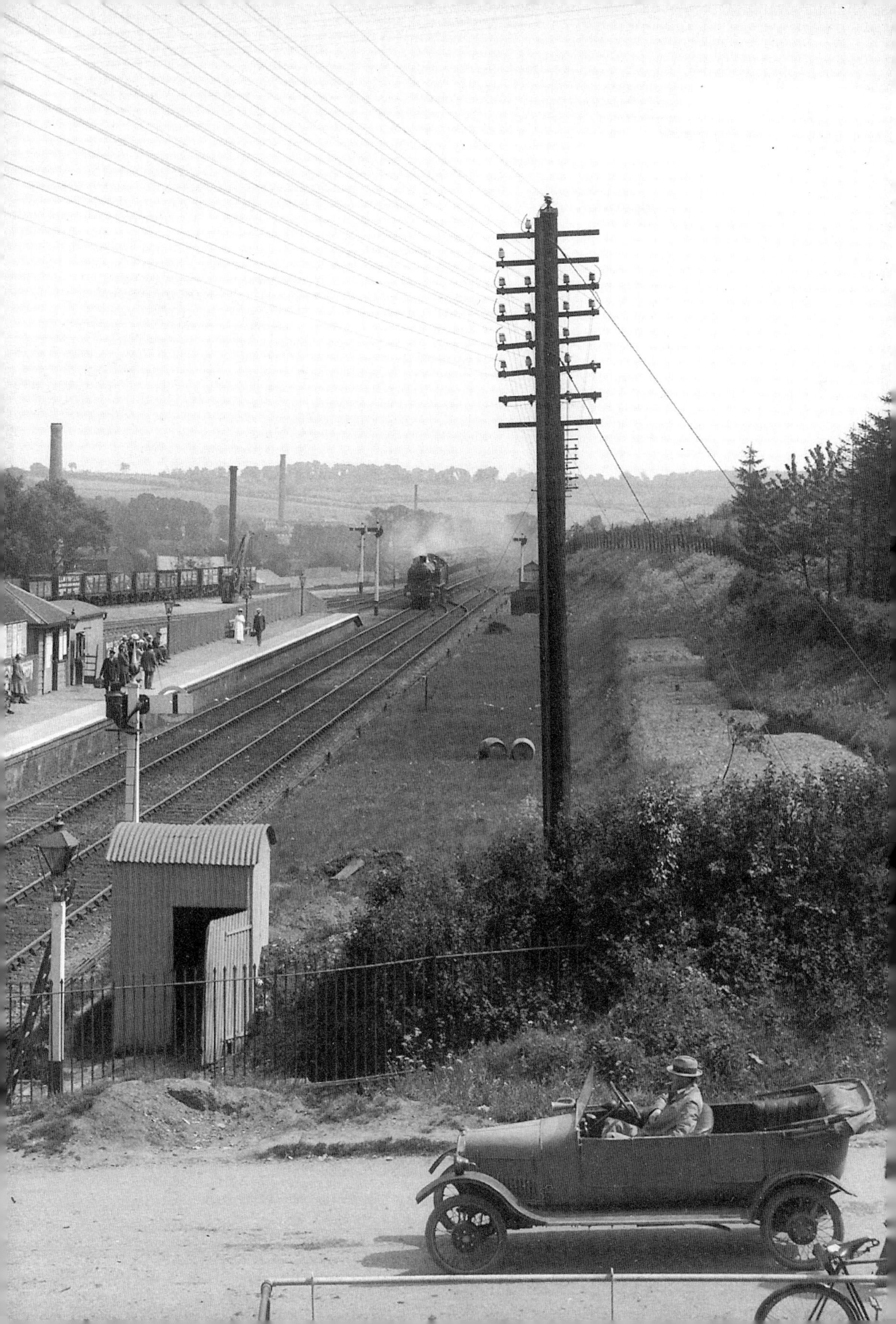

106. The second platform and loop lasted until 1966, but the 25-lever signal box remained in use until the end. A DMU for Bourne End was recorded on 19th January 1969. Goods traffic had ceased on 18th July 1966. (E.Wilmshurst)

HIGH WYCOMBE

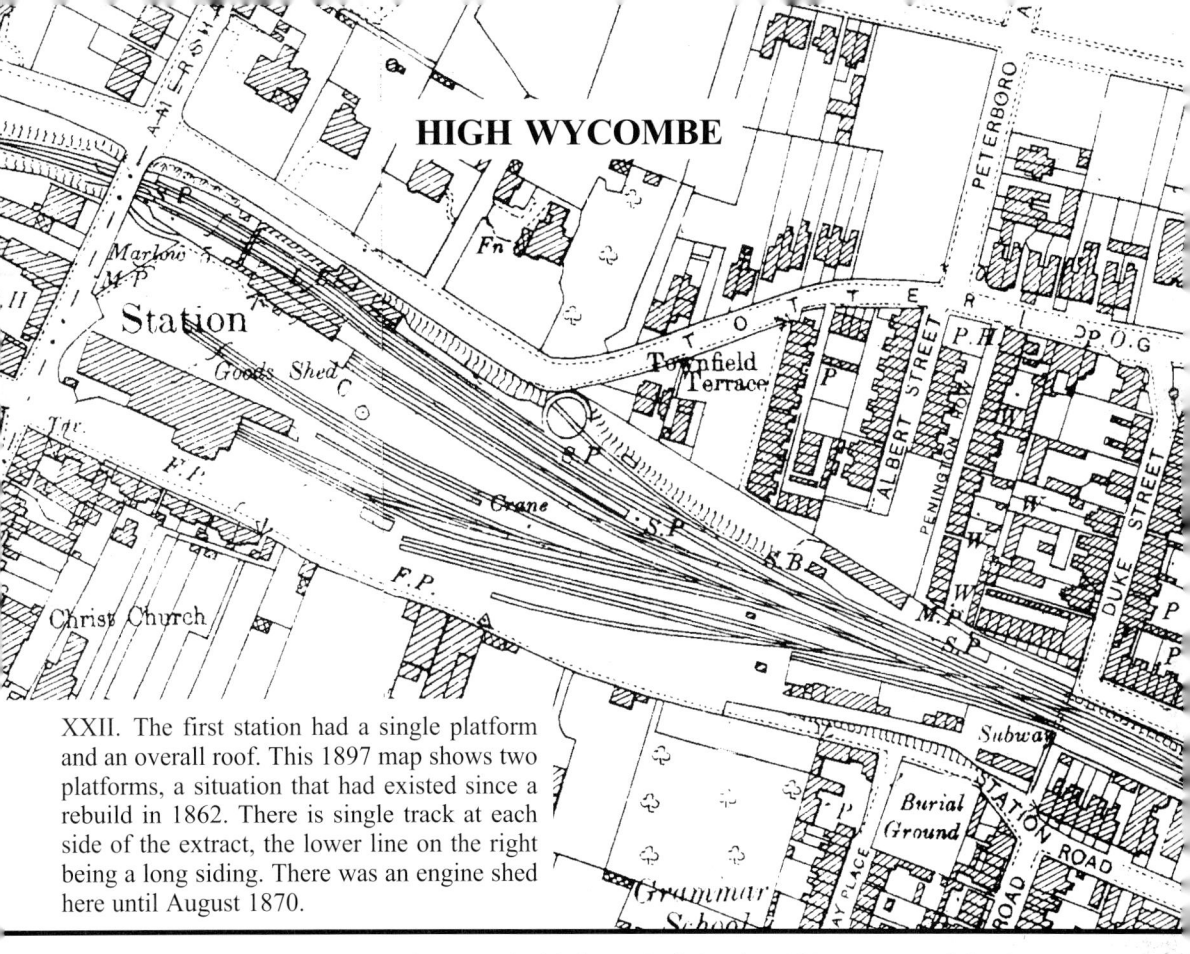

XXII. The first station had a single platform and an overall roof. This 1897 map shows two platforms, a situation that had existed since a rebuild in 1862. There is single track at each side of the extract, the lower line on the right being a long siding. There was an engine shed here until August 1870.

107. The track through the station was doubled on 22nd October 1905, as part of the GWR's scheme to create a new main line between London and Birmingham. This is South Box which was in use from 1905 until 1991 and the separate line for the Maidenhead service is in front of it in this 1932 view. (Brunel University/Mowat coll.)

108. The new station opened on 2nd April 1906 and four tracks were provided through it, plus a bay for Maidenhead trains on the far side of the down platform (left). The bay was still in use in 2001, albeit for direct stopping trains to London. This 1957 view includes the goods yard, which closed in 1966. (B.W.Leslie/GWS)

109. The main entrance, on the south side, was photographed in 1964. The first station had been called simply "Wycombe". The Maidenhead trains ran close to the main line for nearly half a mile. (Lens of Sutton)

4. Marlow Branch
WEST OF BOURNE END

110.   A 1400 class 0-4-2T has propelled its autocoach passed the junction signals on 16th July 1955 and passes over one of three lightly used crossings over lanes leading to the Thames. The autocoach is fitted with steps that could be swung out at the old rail-level halts. (E.Wilmshurst)

111.   The branch has a delightfully rural ambience with trees close to the train as it creeps over the crossings at 10mph (two have lights) and passes quietly over the 50yd long Marlow Viaduct. A marina is close by and pleasure seekers abound. (T.Wright)

MARLOW

112. The terminus had its own distinctive style, being the creation of the Great Marlow Railway Company. This and the next view date from 1921. The milk churns are a reminder of a once important traffic to London. On the left is the coal merchant's office. (LGRP/NRM)

Marlow	1903	1913	1923	1933
Passenger tickets issued	61149	56558	71719	30745
Season tickets issued	*	276	834	1488
Parcels forwarded	35129	48818	34868	25893
General goods forwarded (tons)	9603	3448	915	523
Coal and coke received (tons)	2393	1866	713	1595
Other minerals received (tons)	2080	2994	1731	2717
General goods received (tons)	13486	9584	4760	2618
Trucks of livestock handled	305	433	480	84

(* not available.)

113. Of note from left to right are cattle wagons limewashed for disease control, the lamp hut remote for fire safety reasons, the west elevation used as a source of revenue and the cattle dock, use of which would have impeded engine run-round. The 2¾ milepost is also evident. (LGRP/NRM)

ROBERTSONS
GOLDEN SHRED
CEREBOS SALT
CEREBOS SALT
BEEF TEA
NEWBERY'S FURNITURE READING
Pears'
NESTLE'S MILK
STATION MASTER
G.W.R. HOTELS
CORNWALL
2

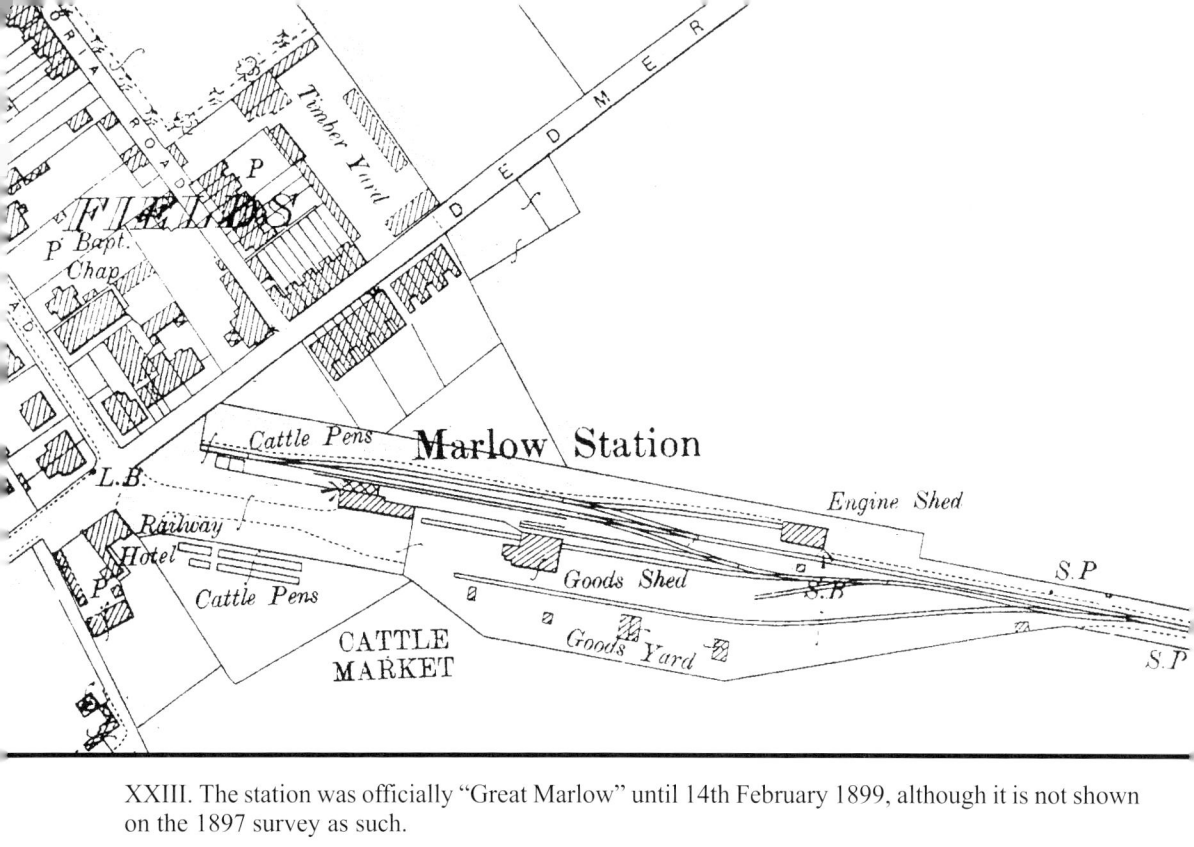

XXIII. The station was officially "Great Marlow" until 14th February 1899, although it is not shown on the 1897 survey as such.

114. We can enjoy two photos from 17th November 1951. This one features the water tank, coal stage, ash pit, engine shed, 16-lever signal box and 2-ton crane, which is in line with the trees. It could have been used for loading the wagons on the right. (A.J.Pike/F.Hornby)

115. No. 1448 waits while the platform is swept clear of puddles. There had been a staff of 13 to 14 in the first 40 years of the century. The gas lamp is still carrying the shade added for the black-out of World War II. The cylinders on the right carry gas of a different type used for carriage lighting but, more commonly, for restaurant cars at that time. (A.J.Pike/F.Hornby)

116. An unusual train was provided for the "Marlow Donkey" for a period, it being this "Clifton Down" set. (R.S.Carpenter)

117. No. 1474 awaits departure sometime after the signals and box had gone. They ceased to be used on 26th September 1954. The engine shed closure followed in July 1962 and its demolition took place in June 1964. Goods traffic ceased on 18th July 1966. The timber yard (centre) had its own siding from 1947; its points are in front of the engine. (R.S.Carpenter)

118. A new platform was built on the south side of the site and opened on 10th July 1967. The former platform line, loop and adjacent siding became the property of J.Davies and were usable until July 1970. (M.J.Stretton)

119. The overpowering Leylandii had produced a depressing environment by the time that no. 165121 was photographed at the end of the line on 12th October 2001. A shelter was provided beyond the platform end. (T.Wright)

120. The access to the platform ramp is to the right of this prison-like shelter; at least it has no glass to break. It often accommodates a person with a portable ticket machine at peak times, as traffic is brisk on this unusual and fascinating link with the past. The service is still known by staff as "The Donkey"! (M.Turvey)

MP Middleton Press

Easebourne Lane, Midhurst, W Sussex. GU29 9AZ Tel: 01730 813169 Fax: 01730 812601
If books are not available from your local transport stockist, order direct with cheque, Visa or Mastercard, post free UK.

BRANCH LINES
Branch Line to Allhallows
Branch Line to Alton
Branch Lines around Ascot
Branch Line to Ashburton
Branch Lines around Bodmin
Branch Line to Bude
Branch Lines around Canterbury
Branch Lines around Chard & Yeovil
Branch Line to Cheddar
Branch Lines around Cromer
Branch Lines to East Grinstead
Branch Lines of East London
Branch Lines to Effingham Junction
Branch Lines around Exmouth
Branch Lines to Falmouth, Helston & St. Ives
Branch Line to Fairford
Branch Lines around Gosport
Branch Lines to Henley, Windsor & Marlow
Branch Line to Hawkhurst
Branch Lines to Horsham
Branch Lines around Huntingdon
Branch Line to Ilfracombe
Branch Line to Kingswear
Branch Line to Lambourn
Branch Lines to Launceston & Princetown
Branch Line to Looe
Branch Line to Lyme Regis
Branch Lines around Midhurst
Branch Line to Minehead
Branch Line to Moretonhampstead
Branch Lines to Newport
Branch Lines to Newquay
Branch Lines around North Woolwich
Branch Line to Padstow
Branch Lines around Plymouth
Branch Lines to Seaton and Sidmouth
Branch Line to Selsey
Branch Lines around Sheerness
Branch Line to Shrewsbury
Branch Line to Swanage *updated*
Branch Line to Tenterden
Branch Lines around Tiverton
Branch Lines to Torrington
Branch Line to Upwell
Branch Lines of West London
Branch Lines around Weymouth
Branch Lines around Wimborne
Branch Lines around Wisbech

NARROW GAUGE
Branch Line to Lynton
Branch Lines around Portmadoc 1923-46
Branch Lines around Porthmadog 1954-94
Branch Line to Southwold
Douglas to Port Erin
Kent Narrow Gauge
Northern France Narrow Gauge
Romneyrail
Southern France Narrow Gauge
Sussex Narrow Gauge
Two-Foot Gauge Survivors
Vivarais Narrow Gauge

SOUTH COAST RAILWAYS
Ashford to Dover
Bournemouth to Weymouth
Brighton to Worthing
Eastbourne to Hastings
Hastings to Ashford
Portsmouth to Southampton
Ryde to Ventnor
Southampton to Bournemouth

SOUTHERN MAIN LINES
Basingstoke to Salisbury
Bromley South to Rochester
Crawley to Littlehampton
Dartford to Sittingbourne
East Croydon to Three Bridges
Epsom to Horsham
Exeter to Barnstaple
Exeter to Tavistock
Faversham to Dover
London Bridge to East Croydon
Orpington to Tonbridge
Tonbridge to Hastings
Salisbury to Yeovil
Sittingbourne to Ramsgate
Swanley to Ashford
Tavistock to Plymouth
Three Bridges to Brighton
Victoria to Bromley South
Victoria to East Croydon
Waterloo to Windsor
Waterloo to Woking
Woking to Portsmouth
Woking to Southampton
Yeovil to Exeter

EASTERN MAIN LINES
Ely to Kings Lynn
Fenchurch Street to Barking
Ipswich to Saxmundham
Liverpool Street to Ilford
Saxmundham to Yarmouth

WESTERN MAIN LINES
Ealing to Slough
Exeter to Newton Abbot
Newton Abbot to Plymouth
Newbury to Westbury
Paddington to Ealing
Plymouth to St. Austell
Slough to Newbury
St. Austell to Penzance
Westbury to Taunton

COUNTRY RAILWAY ROUTES
Andover to Southampton
Bath Green Park to Bristol
Bath to Evercreech Junction
Bournemouth to Evercreech Junction
Burnham to Evercreech Junction
Cheltenham to Andover
Croydon to East Grinstead
Didcot to Winchester
East Kent Light Railway
Fareham to Salisbury
Guildford to Redhill
Reading to Basingstoke
Reading to Guildford
Redhill to Ashford
Salisbury to Westbury
Stratford upon Avon to Cheltenham
Strood to Paddock Wood
Taunton to Barnstaple
Wenford Bridge to Fowey
Westbury to Bath
Woking to Alton
Yeovil to Dorchester

GREAT RAILWAY ERAS
Ashford from Steam to Eurostar
Clapham Junction 50 years of change
Festiniog in the Fifties
Festiniog in the Sixties
Isle of Wight Lines 50 years of change
Railways to Victory 1944-46
Return to Blaenau 1970-82
SECR Centenary album
Talyllyn 50 years of change
Yeovil 50 years of change

LONDON SUBURBAN RAILWAYS
Caterham and Tattenham Corner
Charing Cross to Dartford
Clapham Jn. to Beckenham Jn.
Crystal Palace (HL) & Catford Loop
East London Line
Finsbury Park to Alexandra Palace
Holbourn Viaduct to Lewisham
Kingston and Hounslow Loops
Lewisham to Dartford
Lines around Wimbledon
London Bridge to Addiscombe
Mitcham Junction Lines
North London Line
South London Line
West Croydon to Epsom
West London Line
Willesden Junction to Richmond
Wimbledon to Beckenham
Wimbledon to Epsom

STEAMING THROUGH
Steaming through Cornwall
Steaming through the Isle of Wight
Steaming through Kent
Steaming through West Hants
Steaming through West Sussex

TRAMWAY CLASSICS
Aldgate & Stepney Tramways
Barnet & Finchley Tramways
Bath Tramways
Brighton's Tramways
Bristol's Tramways
Burton & Ashby Tramways
Camberwell & W.Norwood Tramways
Clapham & Streatham Tramways
Croydon's Tramways
Dover's Tramways
East Ham & West Ham Tramways
Edgware and Willesden Tramways
Eltham & Woolwich Tramways
Embankment & Waterloo Tramways
Enfield & Wood Green Tramways
Exeter & Taunton Tramways
Greenwich & Dartford Tramways
Hammersmith & Hounslow Tramways
Hampstead & Highgate Tramways
Hastings Tramways
Holborn & Finsbury Tramways
Ilford & Barking Tramways
Kingston & Wimbledon Tramways
Lewisham & Catford Tramways
Liverpool Tramways 1. Eastern Routes
Liverpool Tramways 2. Southern Routes
Liverpool Tramways 3. Northern Routes
Maidstone & Chatham Tramways
Margate to Ramsgate
North Kent Tramways
Norwich Tramways
Reading Tramways
Seaton & Eastbourne Tramways
Shepherds Bush & Uxbridge Tramways
Southend-on-sea Tramways
Southwark & Deptford Tramways
Stamford Hill Tramways
Twickenham & Kingston Tramways
Victoria & Lambeth Tramways
Waltham Cross & Edmonton Tramways
Walthamstow & Leyton Tramways
Wandsworth & Battersea Tramways

TROLLEYBUS CLASSICS
Bournemouth Trolleybuses
Croydon Trolleybuses
Derby Trolleybuses
Hastings Trolleybuses
Maidstone Trolleybuses
Portsmouth Trolleybuses
Woolwich & Dartford Trolleybuses

WATERWAY ALBUMS
Kent and East Sussex Waterways
London to Portsmouth Waterway
West Sussex Waterways

MILITARY BOOKS
Battle over Portsmouth
Battle over Sussex 1940
Bombers over Sussex 1943-45
Bognor at War
Military Defence of West Sussex
Military Signals from the South Coast
Secret Sussex Resistance
Surrey Home Guard

OTHER RAILWAY BOOKS
Index to all Middleton Press stations
Industrial Railways of the South-East
South Eastern & Chatham Railways
London Chatham & Dover Railway
War on the Line (SR 1939-45)

BIOGRAPHIES
Garraway Father & Son
Mitchell & company